Third Edition

Teaching Reading Skills through the Newspaper

Arnold B. Cheyney

Professor Emeritus
University of Miami
Coral Gables, Florida

ira

International Reading Association
Newark, Delaware 19714

The International Reading Association attempts, through its publications, to provide a forum for a wide spectrum of opinions on reading. This policy permits divergent viewpoints without assuming the endorsement of the Association.

Director of Publications   Joan M. Irwin
Managing Editor   Romayne McElhaney
Associate Editor   Anne Fullerton
Associate Editor   Karen Goldsmith
Assistant Editor   Kate Shumaker

The material in this book is based on a series of columns from the NIE Idea Corner and has been adapted with the permission of the NIE Information Service, a publication of RC Anderson Associates, Pittsford NY 14534, USA.

Library of Congress Cataloging in Publication Data
Cheyney, Arnold B.
Teaching reading skills through the newspaper/Arnold B. Cheyney. − 3rd ed.
   p. cm. − (Reading aids series)
Includes bibliographical references.
   1. Reading.   2. Newspapers in education − United States.
I. Title.   II. Series.
LB1050.c45   1992   91-43174
428.4'07 − dc20   CIP
ISBN 0-87207-236-3

Cover design by Boni Nash

CONTENTS

FOREWORD

Welcome your students to the real world, the world outside the schoolyard gates. Introduce them to the newspaper—the textbook that provides up-to-date information on local, state/provincial, national, and world affairs; the most current analysis and criticism on executive and legislative decision-making; the latest in music, theater, television, and the fine arts; and even columns and comics to make them laugh.

Newspapers are among the most relevant texts available for the classroom. Students like them because they always can find something they care about inside the newspaper's pages. Newspapers are also user-friendly and empowering.

Today's newspapers use design elements—story placement, typeface, graphics—to make information easily accessible to the reader. Important stories usually are placed at the top of a page. The most important stories have large bold headlines. Graphics appear next to related stories.

The text format also presents information in a predictable way. In a straight news story, the headline gives the reader the main idea of the story. The lead paragraph gives a summary of the story in capsule form, answering the important newspaper questions—who, what, when, where, why, and how. The remainder of the news story provides additional details, with the least important information at the end of the story. Opinion pieces such as editorials and columns present an issue, supply facts, and then give the writer's opinions and recommendations.

Newspaper activities empower students by giving them control over their own learning. Students make choices about the content of their lessons. They select the environmental issues to investigate for science class. They select the government leader to study. They select the articles that show the Constitution at work. The teacher chooses the skill, process, or topic, but the students determine the reading material. When students are given these choices, they cannot fail. Using the newspaper becomes a positive and successful experience.

Newspapers teach relevance in a subtle way. Whether students are writing a character sketch of a local artist, computing the cost of groceries for the week, or learning about pollution, the unmistakable message is there: this is *why* we learn to read, this is *why* we learn to compute numbers, this is *why* we learn about scientific processes—this is the real world.

Arnold Cheyney helps teachers build the bridge between classroom lessons and the world outside the classroom door by suggesting specific strategies for using the newspaper across the school curriculum. This book and a newspaper will provide teachers with enough materials to challenge and excite students for hours.

Sherrye Dee Garrett
Lancaster Newspapers, Inc.
Lancaster, Pennsylvania

Why Use Newspapers in the Reading Curriculum?

—— *Why newspapers?* ——

Because they are what adults read most often. People do read books, but in day-to-day life, newspapers make up the bulk of the average high school graduate's reading. Magazines and then books follow in second and third place. (For details on these facts and the statistics that follow, see *91 Facts about Newspapers: A Statistical Summary of the Newspaper Business by the American Newspaper Publishers Association.*)

- **Fact:** On an average weekday, more than 113 million adults in the United States, or 62 percent of the total adult population, read a daily newspaper.

- **Fact:** More than 121 million, or 67 percent, read a Sunday newspaper.

- **Fact:** Each copy of the more than 62 million U.S. daily newspapers sold each weekday is read by an average of just over two people.

- **Fact:** The average reader spends 62 minutes reading the Sunday newspaper and 45 minutes reading one or more daily newspapers.

——— *Why newspapers?* ———

Because teachers can get excellent supplementary teaching aids from their local newspaper by contacting the newspaper's Educational Services Department.

- **Fact:** Almost 700 North American newspapers conduct Newspaper in Education (NIE) programs; approximately 400 sponsor literacy programs.
- **Fact:** Newspaper in Education Week is observed in schools in all 50 U.S. states and the District of Columbia, as well as in Canada and more than 10 other nations.
- **Fact:** Daily newspapers are published in 1,500 U.S. cities, and 93 of these have two or more newspapers.

The American Newspaper Publishers Association (ANPA) Foundation publishes *Bibliography: NIE Publications*, a regularly updated guide that lists more than 300 teacher manuals and curriculum materials related to the use of newspapers in the classroom. The ANPA Foundation also publishes *The Newspaper As an Effective Teaching Tool*, a brief introduction to the NIE idea. (Both of these inexpensive publications are available directly from the ANPA Foundation, The Newspaper Center, Box 17407, Dulles Airport, Washington, DC 20041, USA. For information on prices or ordering, write to this address or telephone 703-648-1000.)

——— *Why newspapers?* ———

Because newspapers have a built-in capacity to motivate readers. When students read, they search for the material's relevance to their lives. When given a choice, they are more likely to want to read the material in the newspaper that describes their school's football or basketball team than the assignment on amoebae in their science text. Poor readers are more apt to carry newspapers—and read them—than textbooks written at their reading level. Students are motivated to find out about events in the world and how they might be affected by what's going on.

Why newspapers?

Because you can introduce your students to the skills of critical thinking, retaining information, and transferring learning to the realities of day-to-day living by using the newspaper as a teaching tool. Through the use of the daily newspaper, students can learn to *read, write, speak, listen, think, interpret,* and *reason.*

Why newspapers?

Because research (see *Educators: Try Me* and *The Newspaper As an Effective Teaching Tool,* both from the ANPA Foundation) indicates that students who study the newspaper in school:

- have greater knowledge of current events;
- are more politically aware;
- know more about the world at large;
- have positive attitudes toward school;
- improve their reading skills and attitudes (as measured by standardized tests); and
- improve in behavior, motivation, and verbal interaction.

So, why use newspapers in reading?

Because they work!

Chapter ONE

Teaching How to Read the Newspaper

There are many ways to present the daily newspaper to your students, but remember that setting goals is of primary importance. Students must come to written words with some indication of what they are going to get from them. The newspaper helps in this quest by presenting information in interesting ways that stimulate readers to read on and encourage them in their desire to know.

Teachers can effectively use the built-in organizational and design features in the newspaper—headlines, pictures, graphics, and so on—in conjunction with their own strategies—advance organizers, analogies, previews, vocabulary instruction, or questions. All this means is that lessons, however simple or complex, must be structured so that students start reading the newspaper with a goal in mind. Preferably, the goal will be their own.

All of the strategies described in this chapter follow this basic format: When students read the newspaper they will (1) set goals for reading, (2) read, (3) relate their past knowledge to the article, (4) think critically about what they have read, (5) form new concepts and understandings from their reading, and (6) set *new* reading goals. This strategy outline is designed to be ongoing so that students' knowledge of current events will grow steadily. The specific strategies described in what follows can be incorporated into this general schema. Students can be told about this basic format so that eventually they will become instinctively aware of the pattern to follow when tackling the newspaper.

Circle of Knowledge

There are three phases in this strategy:

1. posing questions about a newspaper article before the students read it;
2. discussing the questions with the whole class after reading; and
3. activities for summing up.

First, the teacher should select an appropriate newspaper article, one that is right for the grade and skill levels of the students and is likely to interest them. Next, the teacher prepares some questions for the class based on the content of the article. These questions should be broad and general but grounded in the experiences or prior knowledge of the students; if, for example, the article is about civil rights violations in another country, the prereading questions might be linked to the civil rights movement in the students' own country. After the questions are asked, students read the article, jotting down their answers as they do so. They can then use these notes for reference during the group discussion that follows.

For example, say a news article about a coup attempt to overturn a legitimate foreign government prompted these questions:

1. Under what circumstances would it be possible for a coup to happen in this country?
2. How would the citizens, the military, or the current government of this country react to such an attempt?
3. Can you think of any situation in which you would favor a coup in our country?

If the teacher believes that students will have difficulty with the complexity of such questions, they can be allowed to share their thoughts with one another in groups of two or three prior to reading. After a few moments, have the students—individually or still in small groups—read the article.

The postreading whole-class discussion can then take many forms. The students' responses to these questions may lead to a debate about types of government or an exploration of democratic processes. Follow-up work can include assignments of related reading or suggested essay topics (a few activities of this nature will be outlined later).

Reading for Meaning

With this strategy, the teacher poses three questions:

1. **What does the newspaper article say?** This question requires an exact, factual answer. This is the mastery phase—the question leads students to master the article's content.

2. **What does it mean?** This question asks the student to interpret and make an educated guess about the information contained in the article. It is the understanding phase.

3. **What does it mean to me?** This question gets at the heart of what reading is all about. It asks students to apply the information they've read to their own specific experience or situation. This is the synthesis phase.

These three questions can be asked about any written material found in the newspaper: stories, feature articles, sports reports, editorials, letters to the editor, even editorial cartoons. (In fact, they also work well with much of the material frequently found in content area textbooks.) Remind students to direct their reading toward a purpose by putting these questions on a chart in the classroom.

Compare and Contrast

The compare-and-contrast strategy is a three-phase plan that helps students with reading comprehension by teaching them how to organize, critique, and remember information they read in the newspaper.

To understand this information, students establish criteria on which to assess it.

For example, newspapers frequently discuss "hot" topics in their editorial pages and letters to the editor, as well as in articles and features. The teacher can identify an issue that is important to students — say, trying to determine which candidate would be better for a particular office — and assign some newspaper reading based on this issue. Students are told that they will have to discuss their views and decide which candidate deserves to win in the upcoming election.

To discuss this issue intelligently, participants need to agree on criteria. A visual organizer can be displayed, listing the agreed-upon criteria to be used for making judgments. An example follows.

Compare and Contrast: Visual Organizer

Issue: Who is the better candidate — Sarah Yee or Juan Perez?

Criteria	Differences	Similarities
Intellectual Ability		
Political Views		
Past Experience		

In the comparison phase, the students identify the differences and similarities between the two candidates using the criteria they have set and taking their information from the newspaper pieces. The teacher or a student can enter these on the visual organizer as the students make personal organizers at their seats.

In the application phase, the students can use prior knowledge to add to their personal organizers any information they have learned from other sources. At this point, they evaluate the material, come to a conclusion, and express their opinion — perhaps in an essay, a debate, a TV commentary to be read aloud, or in any of the other ways suggested in activities described later in this book.

Synectics

Synectics uses metaphors or the language of imagination to come to grips with the problem of understanding what is going on in the world. Choose a newspaper article for the class to read—say, about a prison where the inmates are holding some guards hostage. Have the students read the article on their own, and then divide the class into small groups for discussion. Next ask the students to write their own versions of what is described in the news story. Then students can go to the chalkboard and write down powerful words that they used in their descriptions.

At this point direct analogies are made. If the word written on the chalkboard is *prison*, an analogy might be "A school classroom is like a prison." Encourage other metaphors that use words such as *hostage* and *knife*.

In the second phase, personal analogy, the students "personalize" these powerful words by trying to view themselves as the objects they describe or suggest. If, for example, one student chooses *hostage* for a personal analogy, he or she could be encouraged to describe the events in the newspaper story from the hostage's point of view.

In the third phase, identifying compressed conflicts, the students develop new analogies, such as "A hostage is a prisoner caught in the confines of the school." Making analogies of what they have read increases students' ability to create imagery, which in turn benefits their writing and speaking. When they encounter new information of the same type they have read, they will have an intensified perception of the material.

Cubing

Cubing is a technique for exploring the meaning found in news articles and feature stories. It consists of six terms (one for each side of a cube) that can be used as a springboard to question material read in the newspaper.

One way to use the technique is to assign each student one of the terms and ask him or her to base a question for the article on that term. Here are the terms and some examples of the questions that could be developed from them:

- **Description:** What is the nature of the problem in this article? How large is the problem? Can you describe it in your own words?

- **Comparison:** Is the problem presented in this article similar to other problems or situations you are familiar with? How is it the same? How is it different?

- **Association:** When you think of the problem in this article, what first comes to your mind?

- **Analysis:** What is your opinion on the extent of this problem in our area of the country?

- **Application:** How could you apply what you learned from this article to your own life?

- **Argumentation:** What position do you take on this article? Are you for or against how it was handled? Why?

An alternative approach is to have each student read an article and respond to it in writing, using these six terms as a framework.

Double Entry

This technique can be used in any setting where material is being read, seen, or heard. It is useful for developing critical reading and thinking skills.

Assign the students a newspaper article to read. Instruct them to make notes on what the article is about on the right side of a sheet of paper as they read. These notes will list the main ideas of the article, perhaps the five Ws (who, what, when, where, why) and how, fragments or phrases from the article, or any specific information that the students deem important.

When they have finished, they scan their notes and react to them in writing on the left side of the same page. Here they can summarize, comment, do freewriting, develop metaphors, or even make up a poem about what they have noted on the right side.

On the next page is a short example of a double entry based on a news article about one of the problems of parking on city streets.

Headline: Downtown Parking Takes a 20 Cent Jump

Second Step: Reaction	First Step: Notes
I don't think that parking fees should be raised. Let's call a strike and meet at city hall.	Parking fees for meters go from 5 cents an hour to 25 cents.
Who cares if the city does need money. I'm a citizen, too.	Fees will generate revenue for financially strapped city.
Parking Meter Haiku If I have to pay More money to park downtown, I'll move to the moon.	"I don't mind paying an extra 20 cents," said Barbara May.

Directed Teaching Lesson

In the traditional directed teaching lesson the teacher talks with the students about the ideas they will find in a particular article of the newspaper. (This assumes the teacher has read the article prior to having the students read it.) Second, the teacher prepares the students for reading by directly teaching the vocabulary in the article that might give them difficulty. The third step is motivation. Here the teacher might prepare questions to be answered, discuss what experiences the students might already have had related to the article, or assign an interesting activity to do at the conclusion of the article. Last, the students read the article silently, complete the assignment, discuss the significance of what they have read, or take a quiz on the article's vocabulary or content.

Note: For more information regarding Circle of Knowledge, Reading for Meaning, Compare and Contrast, and Synectics, contact the Association for Supervision and Curriculum Development (ASCD), 1250 N. Pitt St., Alexandria, VA 22314, USA. Videotapes of these four strategies are also available from ASCD.

Chapter TWO

Reading with Skill and Comprehension

Vocabulary

The acquisition of vocabulary is of great importance in learning to read. If a person doesn't understand the meaning of the words he or she reads, then the skills of decoding, making inferences, understanding story structure, and so on are of little use. Clearly, new vocabulary is not learned in isolation from reading skills; acquisition of vocabulary, however, continues even after other skills have been mastered. The following activities focus on using the daily newspaper to teach new vocabulary, but they should also lead to increased reading competence.

——— *The alphabet* ———

The 26 letters of the alphabet we use in English are the key to opening the door to reading and the world of books and print. In the primary grades, many teachers designate certain days as "letter days." For instance, if a day is designated as *Y* day, students might be encouraged to name things in the classroom that begin with the letter *Y*:

yardstick, yarn, yellow paper, and so on. Older students could use the newspaper in a similar way, perhaps simply to find and learn words containing specific letters.

Once students are comfortable with reading for meaning they can try the following game. The teacher names a topic that fits with the curriculum – say, space, sports, or math. Students are then asked to read the newspaper (either random articles from an entire issue or articles that have been selected in advance by the teacher) and try to find one word that relates to the topic for each letter of the alphabet. If the topic is sports, for example, students might find *archery, baseball, cricket*, and so on through the alphabet. Students should share what they find with the rest of the class, and if a student has picked a difficult or unfamiliar word, he or she should be asked to define it. If a word for a particular letter can't be found, students should try to come up with one, either in discussion or from another source.

——— *Crossword puzzles* ———

Crossword puzzles have obvious value for developing vocabulary. Newspaper crossword puzzles are often difficult, but a teacher may find that, together, the students can fill in five or six items each day. Class time can be set aside to check answers in the next day's newspaper.

Most newspaper crossword puzzles will be much too complex for students in the earliest elementary grades. This does not mean, however, that they can't be used with these young children. Teachers can use the clues in crossword puzzles as a springboard for teaching about synonyms and definitions. They can read each clue aloud (perhaps only once, to help develop listening skills) and ask the children to come up with a response. To become more comfortable with words and word games, students can use crossword puzzles during art time, making designs in the checkerboard patterns or filling in particular boxes in particular colors.

Scavenger hunt

As an introduction to the newspaper, or just as a rainy day activity, try a newspaper scavenger hunt. Make a list of 10 or 20 words you want teams of students to find in one day's issue. (Check to make sure the words you choose are in that edition.) The words can be chosen to emphasize anything you might be teaching at that moment—reading skills (words with the same consonant clusters or vowel sounds), language arts skills (words chosen for their prefixes, suffixes, parts of speech, or alliteration), or content area material (mathematical or geographical terminology, for instance). When students find the items, they can circle or cut them out. The team that finds and can define all the words on the list wins. The ideal situation, particularly in the earliest elementary grades, is for every team to be a winner.

Classifying

This skill is extremely important to daily life. The newspaper is a useful tool for explaining how things can be classified. Start by pointing out how the newspaper is divided into sections, and ask students to list the subgroups found in each section. Then show how the newspaper classifies people by their occupations: for example, baseball players, television personalities, or politicians. Have students cut out all the words naming animals from one day's edition and classify them as pets, zoo or wild animals, or farm animals. Classify the pictures by location or content. Challenge students to find something from a particular category—perhaps an amphibious animal or a mode of transportation. These activities can lead to a discussion of how classifying helps in our daily lives.

Matching

This activity is based on the game "Concentration." Cut out identical pairs of letters, numbers, words, or pictures from two copies of the same day's newspaper. Paste each item on an index card. Mix the cards and spread them out, face down, in a large rectangle. Each child or team tries to make a match by turning over two cards at a time. If the cards match, the child or team keeps those cards; if they don't, the cards are turned back over and the next child or team takes a turn. The individual or team with the most pairs when the "board" is cleared is the winner.

Matching helps develop reading readiness in young children by teaching them to recognize similarities and differences in the patterns of letters and words. For older children the game can be modified to enhance vocabulary acquisition: if the matched cards are pictures, the child must identify the picture prior to removing the pair from the board; if the cards depict a word, the child can be asked to provide a definition or use the word in a sentence.

——— *Foods* ———

Clip pictures of food from the newspaper, along with matching food words. Paste the words on one set of cards and the corresponding pictures on another set. Ask students to match words and pictures. Later, when a large number of cards have been accumulated, have children classify each of them into one of the basic food groups (thereby reinforcing classification techniques learned earlier). Students can also be asked to read about the foods in encyclopedias and locate on a map where they are grown. Target certain vocabulary terms by having children find pictures of foods used to make sandwiches, for example, or of foods found in the school cafeteria.

Difficult words

Choose a column or article from the newspaper that contains vocabulary you think will challenge your students. Ask students to read the piece and write down the words that are difficult for them. Have them try to determine the meanings of these words by working together to use context clues. Then ask them to find the words in the dictionary and write out the correct definitions. Students can also find synonyms for the words and decide if any of them would be appropriate in their sentences. To help them remember new vocabulary, younger students can cut difficult words out of the newspaper and paste them into scrapbooks for later reference.

Denotations and connotations

Choose words from the newspaper, write them on a bulletin board, and discuss the various implications of their meanings. For example, *yellow* is a color between orange and green on the spectrum. In colloquial use, however, "He is yellow" indicates cowardice. The teacher should write words in sentences that illustrate both denotation and connotation and explain how newspapers often use a word's different nuances to make a point.

Function words

Words such as *above, behind, low, top, near, between,* and *up* are best learned initially by linking the physical action with the printed word. Ask the children to roll up tightly several sheets of newspaper in the form of a stick. Have the children place the newspaper above their heads, behind their backs, low to the floor, on top of a desk, and so on.

The students can then try to find the words in the newspaper. They also can use the prepositions to describe the location of different newspaper features in relation to one another (for instance, placement of photos in relation to captions or story).

Question and answer

Students of all ages enjoy finding clues to answer questions or to solve riddles. The newspaper is full of information that can be used to devise question-and-answer games. After reading the front page, a student could make up this one:

Question   Find a word meaning to announce.
Answer   Herald.

Or a student might describe a cartoon character:

Question   This character is around five years old.

The student continues to describe the character until a classmate is able to guess who it is.

Word ladders

To help students develop visual discrimination, have them construct word ladders. Start the word ladder by selecting a word from the newspaper and printing it on the chalkboard.

Say the word is *investigator*; the first student would then have to find a word in the newspaper that began with *r*, the last letter of the word chosen. The student then adds the second word to the chalkboard. That word creates the rung for the next word. Eventually the ladder should look something like this:

investigato*r*
|
*r*id*e*
|
*e*ve*n*
|
*n*ew*s*
|
*s*ubmarin*e*

Continue adding words until there are at least ten. Then encourage children to make their own ladders. Ask them to define any unfamiliar words in their ladders by using the dictionary.

———— *Time words* ————

The newspaper is full of words denoting time. Ask students to cut time words from the newspaper and mount them on 3″ × 5″ cards. Then have them arrange the cards in chronological order. This activity will help students master such things as the order of the days of the week and the months of the year.

Comprehension

Vocabulary development is an ongoing process, but basic strategies for understanding text can be mastered in a finite period. The newspaper, with its varying types of writing, can be a useful tool to promote students' comprehension. Here are a few specific activities that can help.

———— *Sequencing* ————

Sequencing can be taught by having students cut apart the frames of a cartoon strip, mix them, and then rearrange them in correct order. A more challenging task is to have students cut newspaper articles apart by paragraphs, mix these, and then arrange the parts in sequence. This activity can be done individually by students or in pairs if particular attention needs to be paid to analyzing the article. After the students have the article in what they feel is the proper sequence, give them a copy of the original. The students may find differences, but will learn that changing the sequence does not necessarily change the meaning of the article. In fact, the articles are sometimes improved by the students' reordering—a good lesson on why writers should revise their writing.

Drawing conclusions

Students need to learn strategies for weighing evidence and getting at the truth of written passages before forming conclusions. First, they need to determine the premise of an article or editorial: What does the author want readers to believe? Second, readers need to decide on a sentence-by-sentence basis whether they are reading fact or opinion. Have them underline fact sentences in green and opinion sentences in red. Next have students ask themselves whether the facts related support the author's position and whether any pertinent facts have been left out. Finally, based on the evidence given, students should determine whether readers ought to be persuaded to adopt the author's conclusion.

To help younger students learn to draw conclusions from text, pose a variety of questions. Lower level questions center on recall or memorization of data previously learned: Who did...? What led to...? What are...? Tell me in your own words how.... Upper levels focus on analysis and evaluation of data: Why did you enjoy...? What other ending is possible? Why was it wrong (or right) when he did...? Based on our value system, what should they do? Using these questions as a start, help students determine answers to questions relating to text or maybe to their favorite cartoons. Then have them create their own questions. Finally, determine which question are lower level (recall) and which are higher level (analysis).

Cause and effect

Cause-and-effect relationships are prominent in newspapers. For example, one article might relate that a violent storm dumped tons of snow on roads (cause) and that schools are closed (effect). Ask students to find newspaper articles detailing issues such as pollution, inflation, and crime — cause-and-effect situations that touch them personally. Students can review editorial cartoons for simplified presentations of dilemmas and possible resolutions.

Inferring

Learning to draw inferences is of great importance in developing comprehension and critical reading skills. Ask younger students to choose pictures from newspaper advertising supplements. The pictures should depict scenes such as a family eating soup for lunch, or a teenager washing the kitchen floor. Have the rest of the class analyze the implied messages delivered in the ads: that families should eat together, or that teenagers should help with keeping the kitchen clean. Children also can guess what type of product is being advertised. Older students can read newspaper headlines and draw inferences about the nature of the article that follows. After exercises of this sort, the skill of inferring is more easily understood and applied.

Reading aloud

The newspaper contains much material that young students can read to develop oral expression. The advertisements and comics are especially useful for developing this skill. Have each student find five exclamations and five questions from the newspaper. Model examples of change of pitch and phrasing for them so they can hear how to read these sentences expressively.

Older children might enjoy the following read-aloud activity. Divide the class into four groups and assign each group to one of four categories of news: local, regional, national, and international. Each day have the groups prepare short oral readings of the most important stories in their categories. (Have the class determine the criteria for selecting the best stories.) At the end of the week, a panel discussion by each group can highlight the most important stories. Have a Friday "Week in Review" at which students read aloud what they consider the best of the sports stories, comics, features, or book and movie reviews. Or students can present the week's highlights in the form of a TV news broadcast.

Chapter
THREE

Integrating Writing and the Language Arts

In the past, the language arts were broken down into four separate skills areas, each of which required individual attention: listening, speaking, reading, and writing. Further distinctions were made between receptive skills (listening and reading) and expressive skills (speaking and writing). Recently, however, educators have come to approach the language arts in a more holistic way. Such movements as whole language and the process approach to writing indicate an increased awareness of the many connections among listening, speaking, reading, and writing.

This chapter focuses on activities that teachers can use with students throughout the elementary grades to hone writing skills. These activities reflect the newly recognized interdependence of language arts skills. Writing is not an activity to be pursued in isolation from any other skill area. The newspaper, with its many different styles of writing, can be used in a variety of ways to help improve students' facility with all aspects of the language arts.

Getting Ready to Write

In order to be successful and enthusiastic writers, students in the early elementary grades must learn about the techniques that writers use. The following activities are for this "getting-ready" stage and are intended to help show children that using language effectively is not only challenging, but fun.

——— *Print* ———

Newspapers can help students become comfortable with print. Young children can cut apart the large letters found in headlines and re-form them into their own names. These letters also can be used to create greeting and thank you cards, to develop captions for bulletin boards, or to send notes and letters to classmates. Cut out uppercase letters and paste them next to the same letters in lowercase form. Show children how words are made by pasting letters together.

——— *Spelling* ———

If you assign weekly spelling words from a textbook, ask your students to find the words in the newspaper and circle them. This activity can be conducted as a game when the words are first assigned. Give students ten minutes to find as many as they can. This will familiarize your students with seeing the words used in "real" print, rather than reproduced in isolation in their spellers.

——— *Affixes* ———

Knowing the meaning of prefixes and suffixes can help when a reader is trying to understand an unfamiliar word. Encourage students to learn the meanings of common prefixes (un-, bi-, dis-, multi-) and common suffixes (-ment, -ous, -tion). It is helpful to make a chart of common affixes with their meanings so that students have an easy source of reference. Encourage students to find words containing affixes in the newspaper and to notice just how many there are. They then can try to determine the words' meanings without using the dictionary. Have the students practice making new words by adding affixes to common root words.

—————— Compound words ——————

Compound words often develop in three stages — from two words to a hyphenated word to one word (base ball, base-ball, baseball). Ask your students to find ten compound words in the newspaper. Then separate the compounds into two words and write the words in two separate columns. The students can make up other compound words by matching words from one column with words from the other. A dictionary check is vital to determine if they have actually created bona fide words.

—————— Contractions ——————

The newspaper can also help in reviewing the use of contractions. First, define contractions and why they are used. Make sure to explain the difference between contractions and possessives. Then ask students to locate and circle ten different contractions in the newspaper. Have the students rewrite the contractions in both their "contracted" form and as the full words they abbreviate. Then encourage students to write sentences or a page of dialogue using all the contractions they find.

—————— Acronyms and abbreviations ——————

Newspapers are full of acronyms and abbreviations used to conserve space. Some very common words are actually acronyms. Sometimes initials are used to abbreviate a string of words, and the initials become as common as the words they represent (USA, FBI, and UNESCO, for example). Ask your students to find acronyms and words abbreviated by their initials in the newspaper and write them in original sentences.

———— *Parts of speech* ————

Children are usually eager to read the weekend comics. One excellent way to review parts of speech is to circle or underline examples found in the newspaper comics. Use different colored pencils or crayons for each part of speech, beginning with common and proper nouns and then moving to more difficult concepts. Ask your students to put words from each speech category on flash cards and then arrange the cards to create sentences. Use the dictionary to reinforce the lesson that words can sometimes represent more than one part of speech.

———— *Pronoun referents* ————

Pronoun referents abound on the comic pages of the newspaper. To teach this grammatical concept, direct students to underline the pronouns in selected cartoons. Have the students write above the pronouns the antecedents to which the pronouns refer. The students can exchange cartoons and check one another's answers. They can then rewrite the cartoons using the antecedents.

———— *Changing tense or person* ————

The newspaper is an excellent source of practice material for students who are learning to use tense and person correctly in their writing. Have students rewrite sentences from the newspaper in different tenses. For example, if a cartoon character says, "My legs tremble," students could write, "My legs trembled." Search through various stories for verbs and label the tense of each verb found. If material is written in the first person singular, students can change the pronouns to third person singular and note the corresponding change in verb form.

———— *Punctuation* ————

Students need meaningful practice with using punctuation. Assign students the task of finding and circling examples of punctuation marks in the newspaper when specific punctuation concepts are studied (capitals, periods, question marks, and so forth). When students see the way punctuation is used to make reading the newspaper easier, they will be more likely to learn how to punctuate correctly in their own writing.

The comics are a good place for students to practice using quotation marks. Have them choose their favorite comic strip and write out the words in story form. For example, if the words "Stop, thief!" appear in a balloon over a character's head, the student might write:

> Hagar looked up from his dinner and saw his dog running off with a steak. Hagar jumped to his feet and shouted, "Stop, thief!" He then chased the dog up a tree, shook his fist, and called, "See if I ever feed you table scraps again."

Students may find that they have to correct the grammar and punctuation of some cartoons when they rewrite them in this form—an added learning opportunity.

———— *Mistakes, typos, and style* ————

Anyone who has material in print realizes that occasionally slip-ups occur in spelling or grammar, and that typographical errors sometimes elude even the most careful proofreaders. Since newspaper articles must often be produced quickly, they are likely to suffer from such problems. Students enjoy finding these mistakes and typographical errors. Have students find as many mistakes in the newspaper as they can during a five-minute period. Older students can be asked to examine when apparent "mistakes" are really inserted on purpose for reasons of style. Cartoon characters, for example, sometimes speak incorrectly because the author is trying to achieve a certain effect.

Listening

Too often children are *told* to listen but are not taught *how* to listen. Conducting short listening practice sessions each day can pay dividends in the development of listening skills while helping children tune in to language. Read headlines from the newspaper aloud – but backwards. For example, you might read, "Coast east the hits hurricane." When finished, ask the children to write the headline's words in the proper order. Choose short headlines at first and gradually build up to longer ones to challenge students as they become more proficient. This will be easier for them as they become more aware of the parts of speech and the order in which they appear in headlines.

Similes and metaphors

Feature or human interest stories are likely to contain similes and metaphors. First, give a simple lesson on these two figures of speech, explaining how writers use them even in the realistic, informational writing of newspapers. Then have students find examples for class discussion and study. Finally, ask students to create their own similes and metaphors.

Idioms

Many newspaper cartoonists would be out of business if there were no idioms. Hagar the Horrible sends Luckie Eddie to "draw the enemy's fire," for example; Eddie comes back with a drawing of their campfire. Students can learn idiomatic expressions by using them in their own cartoon creations and exchanging the finished products with one another. Here are a few starters: blow your top, kick the habit, give them a big hand, miss the boat.

Literary allusions

Literary allusions are found in practically every issue of the newspaper. Even the characters in the "Peanuts" cartoon strip use them: Snoopy once told Woodstock, for example, that he should not lose his mitten or he wouldn't get any pie. Unfortunately, Woodstock didn't understand the allusion because he'd never heard or read "The Three Little Kittens." Snoopy walked away muttering, "Literary references are wasted on Woodstock."

Point out literary allusions to students and collect them for display on the classroom bulletin board. Demonstrate through these examples that books and stories are interrelated and that reading widely is important to complete understanding of texts.

Students Write

Once students have mastered or at least become familiar with many of the elements and techniques good writers use, they are ready to experiment with their own writing. These activities use the newspaper in inventive ways to show children different styles of and purposes for writing and give them a few ideas for creations of their own.

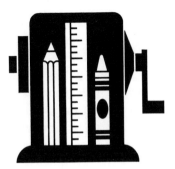

Timed writing

Timed writing is a nonthreatening way to get your students to put pencil to paper. Find interesting articles, comic strips, or pictures in the newspaper. Ask students to examine the material they have chosen, and then have them write about it for ten minutes without stopping. Students should be told that they don't have to worry about punctuation, spelling, or grammar. If they can't think what to write, they can simply restate the action depicted in the material until another idea comes to mind. This exercise will get students used to the physical process of writing and will start them on the road to creative thinking and expression.

Observing pictures

Help your students become better observers and at the same time better writers by asking them to concentrate on a picture in the newspaper and write about its details. The more closely the students look, the more they'll find. Create a contest to see who can find the most details. Soon the students will discover that their writing leads them into a story. Perhaps they could become the main character and tell the story from that vantage point. Much strong creative writing can emerge when students use pictures as a source of inspiration.

Paragraphs

Learning to write a good paragraph is not easy. Practice in asking themselves the five Ws (*who, what, when, where,* and *why*) might help young writers. First, challenge students to find answers to these five questions in the leads (beginnings) of news stories. After the students understand how this type of paragraph is constructed, list the five question words on the chalkboard. Students can think of an event they want to describe and use the five Ws to create an outline for that description. From these outlines, they can write their own paragraphs. At first, encourage students to choose an event from their own experience – a family outing or a sports event, for example – and later have them invent things to describe.

———— *Character sketches* ————

Cartoonists exaggerate character traits – such as quiet, brash, bumbling, neat, foolish, and honest – for comic effect. Students can list the traits of characters selected from the comics and, using this list, can create detailed character sketches of cartoon characters. Once they are familiar with identifying characteristics and writing about them, students can write longer sketches of themselves or family members.

———— *Obituaries* ————

Writing obituaries gives older students a format to follow while practicing writing skills. Students can write obituaries of such things as the family's old car, their faded blue jeans, or a torn magazine. Ask students to include details of how their chosen inanimate subject "died" (a good opportunity for humor!) as well as a "character sketch" of the object.

———— *Letters home* ————

As students read the newspaper, ask them to pick an interesting article that describes the activities of a person they admire. Then ask them to pretend to be that person and write a letter home to their imaginary family, explaining what they are doing. Students will need to read the article carefully, both to determine the nature of the activity and to gain information on their selected person's background. Students can even write a short biography of the person they are pretending to be before beginning their letters so they become completely familiar with the personality they are adopting.

Letters to advertisers

Generally, about two-thirds of a daily newspaper is committed to advertising. Have students skim through the newspaper to find something they or their families have purchased with which they are particularly pleased. Then have them find the address of the company that made the product (this may require some library research and the librarian's help). Students can then list the reasons they like the product and, using this list as an outline, write letters of appreciation to the producer. Mail the letters and wait for the responses.

Advice column

Capitalize on students' natural desire to give advice by patterning an activity after newspaper advice columns. First, list and study with students all the different types of advice columns found in the newspaper: personal, medical, automobile, household, and so on. Note how the problems are presented. Then have the students write problems as they occur to them and slip them (anonymously) into a box. Once a week the teacher can look at the problems privately, removing any that are not appropriate for class discussion and assigning students who are interested in certain areas to write answers for the remainder. A rotating panel of students can review the problems each week and prepare an advice column for a class newspaper.

Dialogue

Most newspaper articles make excellent springboards for writing dialogue among people, animals, or even inanimate objects. Voice can be given to politicians, athletes, and favorite entertainers. For an article headlined "Elephant Hunting Continues in Kenya," students can write out a conversation among the elephants based on the information found in the article: "I hear we're targets for hunters and poachers," says Elephant

One. "Yeah, some of the farmers say we destroy their crops with our big feet," comments Elephant Two. "I think the poachers just want our tusks," growls Elephant Three. With this kind of writing exercise, students learn not only how to write creative dialogue but also how to use punctuation.

———— *Cartoon drama* ————

Cartoons are short dramatic episodes that can be used as the basis for children's plays. First, students can "perform" just the material in the comic strip. They can easily memorize their parts since there is often little dialogue to learn. Let them decide what part each person in their group will play and encourage them to say their parts with expression. As students gain experience in this medium and "get into" their characters they can invent a new dialogue and write a script that extends the scene.

———— *Newspaper poetry* ————

In every section of the newspaper there are sources of ideas for poems. Have students find powerful and picturesque words in articles. Write the children's selections on the chalkboard and use them to form the basis of a class haiku or senryu. (The classical haiku requires a word or theme that indicates a season of the year. The senryu follows the same 5-7-5 syllable pattern but does not require reference to a season.) When children are comfortable with writing in this regulated form, ask them to come up with their own poems.

Editing and Revising

Once students have become comfortable with writing in a variety of forms, it is time to introduce them to elements of revising and editing. Be careful not to do this too early; children shouldn't get the idea that their work is not "right" and has to be corrected or rewritten. The purpose of editing and revising is, of course, to make writing better. Once children are excited about their writing, they will be eager to work on improving it.

Fleshing out writing

Often beginning writers are too economical in their writing, omitting important details or forgetting to include background information. Help make students aware of when they need to include detail by asking them to flesh out the information in newspaper headlines. "New Football TV Deal" gives readers only the bare bones; "The football league signed a new contract with the television network today because they wanted to make more money" tells readers what is really going on.

Next, move on to the synopses of major news articles that often appear on a newspaper's first or second page. Ask students to expand each synopsis based on their reading of the full article. Eventually students can go beyond the article and seek additional material on the topic through interviews, library visits and research, or their own experiences.

Cutting copy

Space requirements often require newspaper writers to drastically shorten their articles and stories. Good writers learn early which material to cut—that is, which details are less important or even irrelevant. Assign students the task of condensing a newspaper article. They can then compare their synopsis with the newspaper's (if one is provided). This activity will help younger students evaluate which details are the most important and will emphasize that good writing is succinct and stays on topic. For older students, this technique can help with précis or summary writing and with making study notes from lengthy reading assignments.

Reordering copy

The structure of a newspaper article has an impact on how interested readers will be in reading it. Putting certain key elements of an article at the beginning or end of the article also can change its meaning substantially. Have students cut a newspaper article apart by paragraphs and then reorder those paragraphs. They will soon see how the meaning has changed or how the material becomes more or less interesting. This is a good introduction to editing, and students will find that it's not as onerous to practice on a newspaper article as it is on their own writing.

Chapter
FOUR

Activities for Social Studies and Science

The goals of instruction in social studies and the sciences include helping students live successfully in a changing world, understand environmental problems, solve problems through critical and creative thinking, and develop individual abilities and interests. The daily newspaper is an excellent and virtually inexhaustible source of information about real-life problems and solutions.

The newspaper can be used in any number of ways to promote learning in the content areas. In general terms, students could be asked to write their own news stories about current events or scientific discoveries using who, what, when, where, why, and how questions, or they might like to try writing biographical sketches of world leaders or famous scientists. No matter what form they take, however, newspaper-based activities in the content areas should promote learning through the process of inquiry. These steps are essential:

- Raise questions about material in the newspaper that relates to social studies or science.

- Have students identify the problems.
- Direct them in gathering data and investigating that data.
- Help students review the data and come to a conclusion.

Some specific suggestions for using the resources of the newspaper in science or social studies lessons follow.

Social Studies

These activities can be used to supplement various aspects of the social studies curriculum. Because of the broad nature of social studies (including history, geography, political science, and economics), only a few suggestions can be given here. It will be demonstrated, however, that the newspaper can be used to complement instruction in a variety of ways that will help bring social studies topics alive for students.

——— *Historical newspapers* ———

The material in today's newspapers probably will wind up in a different form in someone's history text some time in the future. Dramatize this concept by having students rewrite information from their history books in newspaper style. Students can pretend to be reporters or staff writers working at the time of the historical period they are studying. Their writing can take any of the forms found in modern newspapers: a feature story headlined "Lincoln Assassinated"; a weather report titled "Vesuvius Rumbles—Eruption Possible"; an editorial about women's right to vote; or even advertising copy advising readers to trade in their horse and buggy for a brand new Model T. This is a good writing activity, and it will also help bring home the fact that history happened to real people, for whom those happenings were current events.

———— Cities ————

Practically every page of the daily newspaper contains the names of several cities. Young children can cut out these names and pin them to the appropriate places on a large map of the world. The city names can also be categorized under states, countries, or continents. Another option is to write the names on the chalkboard in scrambled order and ask the children to unscramble them and list them in alphabetical order. Activities like these help make children comfortable with print as well as familiarizing them with names of places around the world.

———— Sports geography ————

Help make geography interesting for students by linking it to professional sports. Ask students to write on a large map the names of teams beside the cities in which they play. Ask them what teams are located in certain geographic regions, such as near the Atlantic Ocean, Pacific Ocean, or Great Lakes. What direction will a favorite team fly this weekend to get to its game? What areas will the teams fly over? Which game is farthest north, south, east, or west? How far will a favorite team have to travel? This activity can serve as an introduction to notions of direction, distance, time zones, and latitude and longitude.

Geography folders

Encourage older students to keep a folder or envelope of geographic data gleaned from the newspaper. They can collect stories about where certain events take place in the world and cut out various local, state, national, international, and statistical or demographic maps. When they have gathered sufficient information about a specific area, they can share it with the class. This can help make students aware of the vast differences in our world while at the same time putting geography in some sort of context.

Countries

Certain countries are in the news frequently. Have students select a country to read about in the daily newspaper for one week. Each day, students should clip out all the news and feature articles that appear about their country and keep these clippings in a folder. On Friday, ask students to report what they've learned about their country; perhaps its government policies, economic system, weather, or events that have taken place there. Encourage students to supplement the information from the newspaper with encyclopedia material for more detailed reports. This activity should help students get used to the idea that newspapers are an excellent source of information of all kinds.

Different cultures

The newspaper talks about people of different cultures from all over the world. Ask students to take a section of the newspaper and determine which articles focus on different cultures or people of various ethnic backgrounds. Have them keep track of what type of articles or editorials deal with cultures. Do this for a week to determine whether there is a pattern of reporting about any particular groups. Students will probably find that references to cultures and ethnicities permeate much of the newspaper. This activity can lead students to do more research or conduct discussions about civil rights, domestic policies on immigration or education, and economic issues. Remember that early in their study, students will need to define terms such as culture, ethnicity, race, and citizenship.

——— *Careers* ———

Working in groups of two or three, ask students to find the ten most interesting or unusual careers mentioned or described in that day's newspaper. Ask students to rank the careers in order of their importance to the community and then explain why they ranked them as they did. Next, ask them to categorize the careers in different ways—the amount and kinds of education needed to perform that career, the ways in which that career helps others, and what personality traits they would need for that particular career.

Next, study the classified ads with the whole class. List on the chalkboard available jobs, the duties required, and the salaries paid. Students can make up other categories, including experience necessary, education required, and so on. Figure out the percentage of available jobs that require a high school diploma. Students will quickly see how useful an education is!

——— *Personalities and VIPs* ———

The daily newspaper is full of the famous and the not so famous. Have younger students cut out pictures of various newsmakers and paste them on cardboard. Underneath the pictures students can list the names of the personalities, the reasons they are in the news, and other pertinent information taken from newspaper articles. After several pictures have been collected, students can categorize the personalities and VIPs by occupation: politics, entertainment, or sports, for example.

Older students can keep folders on selected personalities, adding new material as it appears in the daily paper. These personalities may become the focus for studying careers, the subjects for writing biographical sketches, or participants in make-believe interviews. Students in the upper-elementary grades can begin to develop critical reading skills by reading editorials and feature articles about selected personalities and evaluating what the newspaper is saying: What is the writer's opinion of this person? How do you know? Is this opinion justified? Why or why not?

Values

Personal choices in such things as language, clothes, food, vacations, and friends reflect individual, social, and cultural values. The newspaper is a mirror of many values. Discuss with students what they value and have them read through selected newspaper articles to determine whether their values are the same as those of the people in the newspaper. Particular attention can be paid to the editorial and opinion pages. Ask students to describe how their values compare with those they find in the paper. Then have them try to find expressions of certain values (such as courage, dependability, honesty, kindness, patriotism, and responsibility), or lack of these expressions in the articles they read.

Concepts

Concepts such as power, freedom, politics, institutions, justice, and conflict can be expressed and interpreted in many different ways. Understanding the various implications of such notions is crucial because they provide frameworks around which much knowledge is organized. After discussing the meanings of concepts such as these, ask students to find newspaper articles that discuss one or more of them in some way. Students can then share their findings with the class and talk about how concepts have different meanings in different situations.

——— *Issues* ———

The newspaper is full of issues: the death penalty, raising taxes, airline safety, wearing seatbelts, and so on. In order to help students learn about how to evaluate different sides of an issue, try a classroom debate. Students can read newspaper articles to learn the background of an issue and look at editorials to determine where the arguments lie. Next they should clarify their own positions and prepare presentations to state their opinions. This is also a good lesson in the power of persuasive writing and speaking since students can see whether their presentations convince their classmates.

——— *Social problems* ———

Have students identify some of the major social problems affecting their home town. They can collect background material by reading the local newspaper or interviewing people in their community. Then have the students write essays on the topics they have chosen, either describing the problem, arguing one side of an issue, or proposing a solution.

A certain problem can be selected for the students to focus on, particularly if it suits the curriculum. If, for example, you are teaching a unit on family, you can ask students to investigate the special needs and concerns of single-parent households or of senior citizens.

——— *Government* ———

The newspaper is a rich source of information about what goes on in government. Encourage students to collect articles about local, state or provincial, and national governments and use these to determine the responsibilities of various levels of government. Ask students to select one politician and track his or her activities for a week or two. This might involve plotting on a map or globe the travels of the U.S. president or recording the election campaigning of a provincial premier. Clip out, display, and discuss newspaper articles that show government in action — debating issues, enacting laws — and illustrate how those actions can affect citizens' everyday lives.

———— *Rights and freedoms* ————

The rights and freedoms guaranteed to most people who live in democracies simply do not exist in many places. Freedom of speech, the press, assembly, and the right to a fair trial or to own property are taken for granted by many. Emphasize to students how important these rights and freedoms are by having them clip articles from the newspaper that describe places where such liberties do not exist. Next, ask students to clip articles about infringements on these rights and freedoms in the domestic arena, and note the responses to those infringements. This activity should help students learn just how important their rights and freedoms are in real life and teach them about their responsibilities as citizens in upholding them.

Science

Important scientific breakthroughs and science-based issues that affect all of us often are reported in the daily newspaper. Reading about them in this medium, rather than solely in science textbooks, should help students realize that far from being abstract and irrelevant, science is important in day-to-day life.

Weather

Many newspapers publish a map that shows the weather conditions in a very large area. From this map, students can learn to track storms, predict the kind of weather that might occur in various regions in the next few days, and learn general map-reading skills as well. Have students determine the weather conditions and temperatures in a variety of places, perhaps where friends and relatives live. This can supplement a science unit on weather or the seasons.

Pollution

Have students list various kinds of pollution: air, noise, toxic waste, acid rain, and water, for instance. Ask students to read newspaper articles about pollution and determine what, if anything, is being done to solve a particular pollution problem. On a chart, write the headings *Problems* and *Solutions*. Under each heading students can write about the problems and the solutions being offered to combat them. On another chart, list the ways pollution affects the average citizen. On classroom maps, indicate where pollution problems are the greatest in different regions of the world. Activities such as these will help students with classifying and problem-solving skills while making them aware of the huge environmental concerns we all must address.

Space

Encourage students to collect news items and stories about the exploration of space. Space scientists, physicists, and astronauts make excellent subjects for biographical writing and are often profiled in the newspaper. Have students read articles describing satellite launchings and determine how this technology affects them. Remember to teach the specialized vocabulary of space first!

Medical news

For older students, medical news from the newspaper is a good tool to teach classification. Collect newspapers for a week or two. Ask students to clip from the newspapers any items that deal with the topic of medicine or health. (Some newspapers have special weekly health pages or sections.) Have students classify the items they clip by topic—medical research, advances, technology—or by disease. Arrange the clippings on bulletin boards, in class scrapbooks, or in individual folders. Ask students to write reports on a health-related topic, using the newspaper clippings and library research to gather information.

Newspaper accounts about ways to prevent medical problems make excellent discussion materials for health lessons. They can also be used with older students as a springboard for discussing the manifestations of various medical conditions, and with students of any age to correct misconceptions and dispel potential prejudices.

Chapter FIVE

Teaching Mathematics with the Newspaper

At first glance, the newspaper seems to contain little relating to mathematics; a second look, however, makes one realize how much of the language of mathematics is used in daily life. Just looking back on the previous sentence gives an indication of the prevalence of mathematical expressions: the words *first, little, second,* and *how much* appear in just that short space, and all of those words have mathematical associations.

Ask students to select a page from the local daily newspaper and list all of the mathematical concepts they find, beginning with the page and section number and including words with relevance to mathematics, such as penny, telephone number, reduce, five minutes, 2:30 p.m., $200, school year, golfing fees, census figures, and fax numbers. The newspaper also relies on expressing mathematical concepts with figures, charts, formulae, geometrical shapes, graphs, tables, and symbols.

Just a quick glance through the daily newspaper should begin to convince students that knowing about mathematics can help in the real world. Here are a few activities to reinforce that idea and bring the message home.

——— *Quantity* ———

By using the daily newspaper, you can teach the concept of quantity in a variety of ways. Instruct students to circle sets of items in newspaper photographs: cars, people, or animals, for example. Then ask them to count the number of each item in that particular set. Show students two different photographs containing similar items. Ask them to list, count, and compare the items in the selected categories.

Later the categories can be changed to reflect mathematical concepts: cut numbers and number words from the newspaper and have students place them in categories such as fractions, money amounts, units of time, and cardinal and ordinal numbers. Students can also be asked to find the headline that contains the most words or letters or to circle instances of quantities of tens, hundreds, thousands, and millions in selected articles.

——— *Numbers* ———

The newspaper is an excellent tool for showing students the importance of numbers and helping them develop a sense of numerical sequence. Have students circle all the instances of numbers in a given article or newspaper page. Show them the differences between cardinal numbers and ordinals and have them put the numbers they found in sequence. Point out how often numbers that appear in the newspaper denote amounts of money. When children become familiar with numbers, they can make note of the way they are used—to number the newspaper's pages, to indicate weight or height, to give the value of world currency, to predict the day's temperature, to tell what time an event occurred; and so on.

Comparing

Educated consumers know how to compare prices. The newspaper has many advertisements that can form the basis for comparisons. Ask students to find two supermarket advertisements and list and compare the prices for specific quantities of meats, vegetables, grain, and dairy products. This can serve as an introduction to the mathematical notions of less and more. Being aware of the prices of clothes, cars, tires, and other items will help students understand the concept of the cost of living and the importance of shopping wisely.

In addition, students can be introduced to various consumer columns and publications that offer quality and cost comparisons. They can compare job salaries and hourly wages listed in the want ads for jobs requiring little education, a high school diploma, and a college degree.

Adding and subtracting

The newspaper provides many opportunities for practice in adding and subtracting. Ask students to skim through newspaper advertisements to make a "wish list" of things they would like to have. Ask them to add the costs of the items. Next, have the students determine which three or four items on their lists they want least and subtract their cost from the total. This should help put the abstract notions of addition and subtraction into concrete terms for young students.

Older students can use the newspaper to compute the difference between the local high and low temperatures for a particular day, the running time of two movies, or the cost of front row theater tickets as opposed to balcony seats. Students can also list favorite foods and determine the total cost of a meal made up of those foods.

Averages

The newspaper has many practical applications for teaching

the concept of averaging. Let each student select five homes, townhouses, or condominiums from the real estate listings and determine the average price. If births are listed in your newspaper, have students keep track of the number of babies born each day for a month. Determine which day averaged the most births. The weather news can provide information for determining average temperatures or rainfall in a region, city, or town.

—————— *Sports mathematics* ——————

Many students are sports fans and will be motivated to learn facts and figures related to sports. By following sports, students learn the utility of numbers in measuring and predicting success. In basketball, figures commonly discussed include the number of points earned by each team member, the percentage of times a player makes attempted foul shots, the players' heights, and the salaries paid to professional players; in football, observers calculate points for touchdowns and field goals, the average weight of the defensive line, and the distance a team has to travel to play a game. Baseball is a game full of statistics. Ask students to calculate batting averages, earned run averages, slugging percentages, and the number of strikeouts, walks, and balks in a game. Golf and tennis have their own numbers. This sort of exercise will help students realize that mathematical concepts have relevance to things they care about.

—————— *Travel math* ——————

Another activity could be based on the travel section of the newspaper. Students could compute the cost of a week-long vacation to various spots in the world. The cost of food, lodging, entertainment, gas (if traveling by car)—or train, bus, or airfare—and miscellaneous expenses such as taxi travel to and from the airport and tips should be tallied. Students can then compute the average cost per day for their vacation. Compare the various costs of tour packages to make students aware of the different types of travel available at a range of prices. This activity can be used to combine a lesson on math with one on geography.

Problem solving

Problem solving in mathematics is generally more difficult for students than basic computation. The newspaper is full of ideas for creating real problems to solve. Have students look in the classified section to find information on the per-word cost of placing an ad. Students can then write their own ads and determine how much it would cost to run it once, twice, or for a week. Students can scan the advertisements for clothing and determine how much it would cost to replace every item of clothing they are wearing. What would be the lowest price? The highest?

You can also look for stories that talk about budgets or fines and help students work out problems based on the information given. How much is a particular school district spending per student enrolled? How long would a person have to work at a certain hourly rate to pay off a $1,000 fine? Students often find such math problems easier to solve when they are based on real life situations.

Groceries

Help make your students into smart consumers. Ask them to bring in the cash register receipts from their family's recent trips to the supermarket. With these in hand, students can read through newspaper food advertisements and observe if the same items were available for less money at other stores. Then they can calculate the amount of money their family would have saved or lost by shopping at another store. Once they have determined the best place to shop, they can calculate the savings they would accrue by shopping there for six months or a year. Older students could factor in the cost of driving from home to the various markets, based on the average cost of gasoline, the miles or kilometers their family car gets to the gallon or litre, and the distance to the various stores.

—————— *Dream house* ——————

Ask students to figure out the cost of owning their dream house. A study of the real estate section of the newspaper will give them information on the cost of a piece of land, the price of a home, and the terms of a mortgage. Older students can determine the amount of interest on a 20- or 30-year mortgage and how much the monthly payments will be. Selecting the furniture for a home and adding up the cost can be done by examining advertisements. Discuss what appliances may be needed and calculate the price of such items as a television set, stove, washer, and dryer. Figuring out the monthly cost of utilities will give students another perspective on home ownership. Encourage students to do part of this study with their parents.

—————— *Television* ——————

Ask students to skim through the newspaper television guide and note the programs they watched the previous day. Ask them to list the programs along with their lengths in minutes. Then have them add these figures and divide by 60 to determine the number of hours they watched TV. Have students keep track of their TV watching in this way for a week. After they calculate their weekly viewing time, have students project the average number of days per year they spend in front of the television. Then try to encourage them to spend at least some of that time reading instead!

—————— *Tables and schedules* ——————

Tables and schedules permeate the newspaper. Advertisements list items and their prices; the movie section provides schedules; television listings include channels, times, and programs; the sports pages list batting averages and football scores; and the business section lists stock market quotations. Help students become aware of the ways numerical concepts can be expressed in tables and schedules by dividing the class in groups to discuss how a reader gains information from such lists. Each group can look at one table or schedule or at several examples of the same type and then explain to the rest of the class how they can be read.

Graphs

Graphs put large amounts of information into a visual and easily comprehensible form. After teaching an introductory lesson on graphs and graphing, you can have students make their own with grid paper and the newspaper comics. On the grid, students number from 1 to 30 vertically on the left side; across the bottom, students write the names of the cartoons. Then they can graph the number of words in each cartoon strip in bar graph form. Graphs can also be created for the number of pages in each section of the paper, the number of words in headlines, daily temperatures for a week, and the number of people pictured in each section. Older students can link graphing to studies in other content areas. They could, for example, graph the number of times a particular political figure gets his or her name in the newspaper or the frequency of stories about pollution in a certain area.

These and other activities can help students hone their math skills while teaching them to read critically. As with any instruction, teachers should use discretion in choosing or adapting classroom activities to meet their students' particular needs. In the hands of discerning teachers, the newspaper can be an excellent tool to further students' understanding of society, as well as their scholastic abilities in a wide range of disciplines.

EASY PEASEY

People Skills for Life

Pease International

Copyright © Allan Pease 2006

Published in Australia in 2006 by Pease International Pty Ltd.,
29 Crosby Hill Road, Buderim, Queensland 4556 Australia

info@peaseinternational.com
www.peaseinternational.com

ALLAN & BARBARA PEASE

Australian Library Cataloguing-in-Publication Data

A catalogue record for this book is available from the
Australian Library

ISBN-13: 978-1-920816-16-X
ISBN-10: 1-920816-16-X

Easy Peasey – People Skills for Life

Barbara & Allan Pease

Illustrated by John Hepworth
Cover by Bonny Morlak
Text design and typesetting by Bookhouse, Sydney

Printed and bound in Australia by McPherson's Printing Group

Acknowledgements

Here are some of the people who contributed directly or indirectly to this book, whether they knew it or not:

Ray & Ruth Pease, Dr Dennis Waitley, Trevor Dolby, Malcolm Edwards, Ron & Toby Hale, Deb Mehrtens, Jim Cathcart, Steve Wright, Trish Goddard, Kerri-Anne Kennerley, Bert Newton, Leon Byner, Ron Tacchi, Gerry & Kathy Bradbeer, Kathy Contoleon, Trevor Velt, Kevin Fraser, Alan Garner, Brian Tracy, Gerry Hatton, John Hepworth, Glen Fraser, David Smith, Sally & Geoff Burch, Dorie Simmonds, Decima McAuley, Ian & Jo Abbott, Norman & Glenda Leonard.

Contents

Introduction

We all admire those who seem to have the natural ability to enter an unfamiliar social situation and begin to engage others in conversation. These people have what is often called 'charisma'. While some people wonder how they do it, most assume that they must have a 'natural' talent. The reality is that 'charisma' is an acquired skill of influential people, and like any other acquired skill, it can be learned, enhanced and perfected when you have the right information and the determination to learn.

Easy Peasey – People Skills for Life will provide you with the necessary skills you'll need to become influential with *everyone*. When you put these skills into action, don't be surprised if people begin asking, "Where did you get the ability to talk with people so successfully?" Even if they don't ask, they'll certainly be thinking about it, just as you once did.

This book is about the essential skills that achieve extraordinary success with everyone. We've designed it so that you can open it at any page and start learning a new skill instantly. You'll notice that we get straight to the point with each skill, give an example and then finish. Just like this introduction.

Allan & Barbara Pease

The Three Fundamentals of Human Nature

1. The Importance of Feeling Important

The greatest needs of human nature are to feel important, to be recognized and be appreciated

                                              – Thomas Dewey

The human need to feel important has been found to be higher than physiological needs such as hunger because after a person has eaten, they are no longer hungry. The need for feeling important is even higher than the need for love because when love is attained, the need is satisfied. It's also higher than safety because when a person is secure, safety is not an issue.

The desire to feel important is the strongest constant human urge and is the one characteristic that separates us from the animals. It makes people want to wear brand label clothing, drive upmarket cars, have a title on their door or brag about their children. It's the

main reason kids join street gangs. Some people will even become stalkers or murderers in their pursuit of notoriety.

Marriage studies have found that the prime reason women leave long term relationships is not because of abuse, cruelty or domination – it's because of lack of appreciation. The desire to be recognized, to feel important and appreciated is all-powerful. And the more important you make someone feel, the more positively they will respond to you.

2. People's Primary Interest is in Themselves

Others are far more interested in themselves than in you, so your main goal when talking with them is to talk *about* them.

For example, you should talk about

their feelings
their family
their friends
their status
their needs
their opinions
their possessions

and never about *you* or *yours* – unless they ask.

In other words, on a basic level, people are only interested in themselves and 'what's in it for them'. To successfully relate to people, you must approach them with this rule being the basic foundation stone of human relations. And if someone doesn't ask about *you* and *yours*, they're simply not interested, so don't bring it up.

Some people are disappointed at this basic principle of human nature and see others as selfish and self-possessed because it's fashionable to believe that we should give of ourselves with no expectation of return. Most people who give completely selflessly understand the basic law that "what you give will be returned to you in some way, at some other time, plus interest." The reality is that **every** act we perform in life is motivated by self-interest. Even the donation you made to your local charity was motivated by self-interest and the feeling of generosity you felt when giving. The bottom line is that *you* received the ultimate payoff, even if you did it anonymously. Mother Teresa gave her entire life to others so that she could feel fulfilled in herself by making God happy. And all these actions are positive, not negative.

People who expect others to act in ways other than primarily for their own interests are continually disappointed and feel 'let down' by others.

There is no need to feel embarrassed about this or apologize for it – it's simply the way life is. Doing things for ourselves is a survival instinct that is hard-wired into our brains and has been a characteristic of humans since the beginning. It's the basis of self-preservation. Understanding that we all put our own interests first is one of the keys for any successful venture in dealing with others.

Practice making people feel important through recognition and appreciation every day for thirty days, and it will become a habit that will come naturally to you forever.

---

3. Nature's Law of Equal Returns

This is an irresistible subconscious urge to return to the giver, something of equal value to what was given. If a person likes what

you give them, they will want to reciprocate by giving or doing something that you will like. For example, if a person receives a card from someone they haven't sent a card to, they feel an urge to quickly try to respond.

When you do someone a favor they will usually watch for the opportunity to reciprocate. If you pay someone a compliment, they will not only like you, they will try to return it. If you seem aloof or distant however, they will perceive you as unfriendly and they'll behave in an unfriendly way. If you are dismissive, you may be considered rude or glib and they'll respond to you in a similar way. If you insult them, they feel the urge to return the insult. But when you put out something positive, you will, at some point, receive a positive in return. When you put out a negative however, you will receive in return a much *greater* negative than you gave. This is a Law of Nature, and it rarely fails.

To be popular, always make people feel more important than you in some way. If you act as though you are better, they will feel inferior or jealous. This is counter-productive to building positive relationships.

For example, any time you are served an excellent meal at a restaurant, or a shop attendant asks how you are, or the cleaner at the airport takes away your dirty dishes, smile and make a point of thanking them for their courtesy.

When you understand and accept these three fundamental aspects, you will be amazed at the power you will have in influencing others.

Summary

1. **The highest urge of human nature is to feel important and to be appreciated**
   - The more important you make someone feel, the more positively they will respond to you.

2. **People's primary interest is in themselves**
   - Approach others from a position of what *they* think and what *they* want.

3. **Nature's Law of Equal Returns**
   - Whatever you give out, you will receive back in multiples sometime, somewhere.

SECTION A

Making People Feel Important

1

How to Give Sincere Compliments

Research shows that when you compliment others, you are likely to be seen as sympathetic, understanding and attractive. So, compliment your partner, your colleagues, your employees, your boss, the person you just met, your customer or client, the postman, the gardener, your children. Everyone! There is something about *every* person that you can notice and compliment, however small or insignificant it may seem to you. We guarantee that if you regularly try to make everyone feel special, a new and different world will open up to you.

The most common way to express admiration is to deliver a Direct Positive compliment. This type of compliment tells someone, in a straightforward manner, what you appreciate about their *behaviour, appearance* or *possessions*.

For example:

Behaviour: You're a good trainer.
Appearance: You have a nice hairstyle.
Possessions: I like your garden.

Of these three compliments, a compliment about a person's behaviour has been shown to have the most persuasive effect. Compliments like these become powerful with two techniques:

1. Using the person's name

Using a person's name creates a greater level of interest in the conversation and causes them to listen intently to any statement that follows. Any time you make an important point, preface it with the listener's name and the attention given to that point and how much they remember are significantly increased.

2. The *What/Why* technique

Most compliments fail because they state *what* they like but don't explain *why* they like it. The power of the compliment depends on its sincerity; only telling the person *what* you like often sounds like flattery and doesn't work. Always say *why* you like it. For example:

> Behaviour: '*Alan,* you are a good trainer _because_ you give each of us your personal attention.'
>
> Appearance: '*Sue*, you have a nice hairstyle _because_ it highlights your eyes.'
>
> Possessions: '*John*, your garden is beautiful _because_ it blends perfectly with the environment.'

Become a name user, tell others *what* you like and *why* you like it and they will remember you and what you say for a longer period of time. Never pay a compliment if you really don't mean it. That's flattery and is easy to spot. Flattery is telling another person exactly what he thinks of himself.

Third-person Compliments

These are compliments intended to ultimately reach someone other than the person you are addressing. You can deliver a third-person compliment by making it within earshot of the person for whom

it is intended. You can make the compliment to someone else such as a best friend or the local blabbermouth, in other words, to a person who is likely to pass it on. Praise delivered publicly this way is far more believable and more valuable than praise delivered privately.

Relayed Compliments

This compliment involves someone else mentioning that he likes the behaviour, appearance or possessions of another person, and you passing on that message.

For example:

"Hey _Bob_ – John tells me you're the best player in the club _because_ you're unbeatable. What's your secret?"

A business person calling a prospect on the telephone for an interview could say:

"_Mr. Johnson_, I hear you're the best accountant in town _because_ you get results. Is that true?"

This relieves tension and usually gets a laugh.

How to Receive a Compliment

When someone pays you a compliment:

1. Accept it
2. Thank them for it
3. Prove your sincerity

For example:

Kylie: "Your car looks nice, Anne."
Anne: "Thanks Kylie. I washed and waxed it this morning and your noticing makes me feel good! I appreciate it."

Accepting compliments shows others that you have a good self-image. Rejecting a compliment is usually interpreted as a personal rejection of the person giving it.

Make a habit right now to compliment three people every day on their behaviour, appearance or possessions and watch how they react to you. You'll quickly discover that it's more rewarding to give compliments than it is to receive them.

2

How to Listen Effectively

We all know people who are good talkers, but we'd rather spend time with good listeners. A fascinating conversationalist is a person who listens intently whilst the other is speaking.

Good listeners make better first impressions than good talkers. Forty percent of people who see a doctor do so because they want someone to listen to them, not because they're ill.

For the most part, angry customers, dissatisfied employees and upset friends simply want someone to listen to their problems.

To be a great conversationalist, be a great listener.

We can think three times faster than we can listen and that's why most people find it difficult to listen effectively. In business, the first step is to sell yourself and then to sell your idea, product, service or proposition. This stage is known as the 'listening stage'. Your objective is to sell yourself first and then ask relevant questions about your prospects and their needs to uncover their dominant desires or 'Hot Buttons'.

The 5 Golden Rules for Listening

1. Use 'active listening'

'Active listening' is a remarkable way of encouraging others to keep talking and to be sure you understand what they are saying to you.

To use 'active listening' you simply paraphrase what a person says and feed it back to them, starting with the word 'you'.

Here's an example:

> Mark: "My company has 1200 staff, so it's really tough to get ahead."
> Melissa: "You're feeling really frustrated." (active listening)
> Mark: "That's for sure. I go to the job promotion interviews but I don't seem to land the positions."
> Melissa: "You think you're getting the run-around." (active listening)
> Mark: "Exactly. If they don't think I'm up to it, I'd like to be told straight!"
> Melissa: "You want others to be honest with you."
> Mark: "That's right! And not only that...(etc.)"

If you're not sure that you've heard someone accurately, add the words, 'Am I right?' to the end.

For example:

> Melissa: "You want others to be honest with you. Am I right?"

Active listening allows others to talk openly because you are not giving opinions or being critical. It also means that you are never wondering what to say next.

2. Use Minimal Encouragers

When the other person is speaking, encourage them to keep talking by using these Minimal Encouragers:

> I see...
> Uh, huh...
> Really?
> Tell me more...

Minimal Encouragers can triple the length of the other person's statements and the amount of information they give.

3. Keep eye contact with the person

Meet their gaze for the same length of time that they meet yours. Mirroring a person's gaze creates rapport.

4. Lean towards the person as you listen

We lean away from people we don't like or who bore us. Lean forward – show you're interested.

5. Don't interrupt the speaker; stick to the point

Avoid the urgency to change subjects. Let them finish what they're saying.

3

How to say 'Thank You'

To some people, learning how to say 'thank you' may seem trivial but it is one of the most powerful skills in the art of building relationships. Look for opportunities for thanking people wherever possible.

The 4 keys for an effective 'Thank you'

1. Say your thanks clearly and distinctly

By speaking plainly you leave no doubt in the person's mind that you mean your thanks. Be glad you're saying it. When others overhear you giving thanks, it amplifies its effectiveness.

2. Look at the person and touch them

Making eye contact with the person reinforces your sincerity and a light brush on the point of their elbow with your hand will reinforce your thanks and make it more memorable.

3. Use the person's name

Personalize your thanks. "Thank you, Susan" is far more powerful than "Thank you".

4. Send a written 'thank you' note

This is the best 'thank you' when the situation allows for it. A face to face "thank you" comes next in impact, followed by a telephone 'thank you'. And a text message is better than saying nothing.

Be sincere when you thank a person. Let them know your thanks is genuine. If you're not honest about it, your body language will give you away. Become a 'Thank You' carrier. Look for opportunities to thank others about things that are not obvious.

4

How to Remember People's Names

To every person, their name is the sweetest sound in the world. To them it encompasses everything they are and studies show that people listen intently to any sentence following the use of their name.

Most of us don't remember people's names when we first meet them. This is because we are so preoccupied with the impression *we* are making that we don't even hear the person's name. It's not that we forget their names – we actually *don't hear* them.

Here are the 3 steps to developing powerful memory recall:

Step 1. Repeat their name

When you are introduced to someone new, say their name out loud twice to make sure you heard it correctly and this gives you the opportunity to memorize it. If you were introduced to Susan, say "Susan... nice to meet you, Susan." If it's an unusual name, ask them to spell it and this gives you even more time to memorize it.

Step 2. Turn their name into an object

The reason names are hard to remember is that they aren't solid objects that the mind can picture. To recall a person's name, make a picture in your mind of what their name sounds like. For example, 'Barbara' sounds like barbed wire, 'Jack' sounds like a car jack, for 'John' picture a toilet bowl and for 'Kathy' imagine a cat.

Step 3. Create a ridiculous scene

Next, imagine the object interacting in a ridiculous way with a prominent feature that the person has. For example, if Barbara has a larger than average nose, picture her with barbed wire through it and that you are leading her around with it. If Jack has a prominent chin, imagine a car jack under it jacking it up. If John (as in toilet) has a receding hairline, imagine he's wearing a toilet bowl on his head like a cowboy riding the range. If Kathy has three holes in her earlobes from wearing earrings, imagine a cat hanging from her ears by its claws. The secret is – the more ridiculous the scene, the easier it will be to recall.

Pages 20–22 give you a list of the 50 most common men's and women's names and the solid images to use for instant recall. Practice using these images and suddenly everyone will start to think you're a genius. Never tell anyone how you've become so great at recalling names, as you will quickly lose friends – especially when you meet Bruce (a goose) and Jennifer (chin of fur).

Memory keys for men's names

Name	Key	Name	Key
ADAM	A dam, Adam's Apple	JAMES	Jams
ADRIAN	A dream, A drain	JEFF	Deaf, chef
ALAN	Ale, a lens	JIM	Gym
ALBERT	A belt	JOE	Joke, joey
ALEX	Axe, legs	JOHN	Toilet
ANDRÉ	Entree	KEITH	Teeth, keys
ANDREW	Ant drew	KEN	Ken doll, can
ANTHONY	Ant eating honey, anthem	KEVIN	Heaven, cave in
ARNOLD	Arm hold	LARRY	Lairy, lariat
ARTHUR	Author	LOUIS	Louvres, lures
BARRY	Berry, bury	LUCAS	Low kiss
BEN	Bench, bend	LUKE	Luke warm
BERT	Bird	MALCOLM	Welcome, milk
BILL	$20 bill, duck bill	MARK	Marker, marking pen
BOB	Blob, English bobby	MATTHEW	Mat threw
BRIAN	Brain, iron	MIKE	Microphone
BRUCE	Bruise, goose	NEIL	Kneel, nail
CAMERON	Camera	NEVILLE	Never, Devil
CARL	Car, curl	NICK	A nick (cut), neck
CHARLES	Prince Charles, charred	PATRICK, PAT	Hat trick, pat
CHRIS	Xmas, Christ, cross	PAUL	Pole, pail
CLIFF	A cliff, cuff	PETER	Egg beater, heater, peat
COLIN	Collar, cold	PHILLIP	Phillips screwdriver, flip
DAMIAN	Dalmatian	RALPH	A barking dog, raf
DAN	Dance, den	REG	Red, reach
DARRYL	Drill	RICHARD	Rich Heart
DAVID	Davit, Star of David	RICK	Rickshaw
DENNIS	the Menace, dentist	ROBERT	Robber
DICK	Deck	ROBIN	Robin Hood
DON	Donald Duck, donkey	ROD	Rod, fishing rod
DOUG	Dig, dog	ROGER	Rager
DUNCAN	Dunk, dunnycan, dungeon	RONALD, RON	Ronald MacDonald, run
EDWARD	Head of wood	ROY	Royal, toy
EVAN	A van	SAM	Sandwich
FRANK	Frankenstein, frankfurter	SIDNEY	Opera House, sit knee
FRED	Fred Flintstone, frayed	SIMON	Sigh, Simple Simon
GARY	Carry, glory	STAN	Stand
GEORGE	Gorge	STEVE	Sleeve, steep
GERRY	Geriatric, jerry	TED	Dead, bed, Teddy bear
GRAHAM	Grey, grey ham	TIM	Dim (stupid), tin
GRANT	Granite	TOM	Tom cat, tom-tom drum
GREG	Keg, egg, grog	TONY	Toe knee
HARRY	Hairy	WARREN	Rabbit warren, warn
HENRY	Henry the 8th, hen	WAYNE	Whine, weighing
JACK	Car jack	ZACK	Sack

Memory keys for women's names

Name	Key		Name	Key
ABIGAIL	A big ale		JUDY	Judo
ADRIENNE	A drain		KAREN	Carrot
ALICE	Lice, Alice in Wonderland		KATE	Cake
AMANDA	Almond, A man		KATHY	Catty, cat
ANGELA	Angel		KAY	Key
ANITA	Ant eater		KIM	Kimono, Hymn
ANN	Ant, add		LAURA	Lord, lawn
ANNABEL	A new bell		LAVERNE	Love urn
ANNETTE	A net		LINDA	link, lint, lend
AUDREY	A tree		LISA	Leash, lizard
BARBARA	Barbed wire, barber		LOU	A loo, loop
BEATRICE	Beat rice		LOUISE	Leaves
BELINDA	Blind		LUCILLE	Loose ear
BEVERLEY	Beverage		LUCY	Loose
BRENDA	Blender		LYNDEL	Lentil
CARMEL	Caramel		MARJORIE	Margarine
CAROL	Carol, Xmas carol		MARTINA	Martini
CHARLOTTE	The harlot		MARY	Merry, marry
CHERYL	Cherry, chair		MAUREEN	Moron
CHRISTINE	Christen, Xmas		MAXINE	Maximum, Mad Max
CLAIRE	Eclair		MELISSA	Blister, miss her
CLAUDIA	Clawed, claws		MONICA	Harmonica
COLLEEN	Collar, clean		NICOLE	Nick, nickel
CRYSTAL	Crystal		OLIVIA	A lover
DAPHNE	Deaf knee		PAM	Pan
DAWN	Dawn		PAT/RICIA	Pat, pat of butter
DEBBIE	Debutante, deputy		PENNY	Pen, penny
DEBRA	The Bra		RACHEL	Rachet, rake
DENISE	Dentist, the knees		REBECCA	Beckon
DIANE	Dye, Lady Diane		ROBYN	Robin Hood
ELIZABETH	Queen Elizabeth, lizard		ROSEMARY	Rose, a merry rose
EMMA	Armour, hammer		ROXANNE	Rocks
EVELYN	A violin		SALLY	Salad
FIONA	Phoner, foamer		SANDRA	Sand
FLORENCE	Floor		SARAH	Sara Lee
GAIL	Gale		SERENA	Serene, screamer
HEATHER	Heaven, feather		SHIRLEY	Shirley Temple
HELEN	Hell, helmet		SONJA	Song, sonar
JACKY	Car jack, jockey		SOPHIE	Soapy, sofa
JAN	Jam		SUSAN	Soup, lazy susan
JANE	Chain		THERESA	Trees, Mother Theresa
JEAN	Jeans		VERONICA	Fur on her
JENNIFER	Chin of fur		VIRGINIA	Virgin
JESSICA	Chase a car		WENDY	Windy
JOAN	Joan Collins, joke		YVETTE	A vet

Memory keys for common last names

ADAMS	A dam	LAWSON	Law, lawman
ALLEN	Allen key, a lens	LEE	Lei, lay
ARMSTRONG	Strong arm	LEWIS	Louvres
BAKER	Baker, bakery	LIM	Limp, limb
BARNES	Barn	LYNCH	Lynching
BARRETT	Barrow, barrel	McDONALD	Ronald McDonald
BENNETT	Bonnett, bent it	MARSHALL	Marshall, sheriff
BLACK	Plaque	MARTIN	Martini
BRADY	Brandy, Brady bunch	MILLER	Miller, mill
BREWSTER	Rooster, brewery	MOORE	Mower
BROWN	Brown, brownie	MURPHY	Mercy, murky
BURKE	Burp	MURRAY	Marry, merry
BURNS	Burns, burner, sideburns	NEWMAN	New man (price a head)
CAMPBELL	Camp bell, camp	NORRIS	Nurse
CHANG	Chain, hang, shank	O'BRIEN	A brain
CLARK	Clerk, cloak, cluck	PAGE	Bool or magazine page
COLLINS	Joan Collins, collar	PARKER	Parking meter
COOK	Cook, Captain Cook	PEARCE	Pierce
COOPER	Copper, chicken coop	POWERS	Power fist, power tool
DAVIS	Davis cup, davits	PRESTON	Press, a ton-pressing
DICKSON	Duck's son, son of dick	RICHARDS	Rich heart
DOUGLAS	Dug, dog with glasses	ROBERTS	Robber, Robin Hood
EDWARDS	Head wood, head warts	ROGERS	Rods, Roy Rogers
EGAN	Eagle	RUSSELL	Wrestle
EVANS	Heavens	SCOTT	Scotsman
FOSTER	Frosty, Fosters Beer	SIMPSON	Shrimp, Samson
GALLAGAH	Galloper, galah	SINGH	Sing, sink
GRANT	Granite	SMITH	Blacksmith
GREEN	Golf green, greenhouse	STEELE	Steel bar, thief
GRIFFITHS	Grippers	STEWART	Stew, Steward
HAMILTON	Ton of ham	TAN	Suntan, tin
HARRIS	Hairless	TAYLOR	Tailor, tail
HENDERSON	Hen doors	THOMAS	Tom cat, Thomas train
HILL	Hill	TURNER	Tina, fitter and turner
HUGHES	Huge, hues	WAGNER	Wagon, wagging tail
HUNT	Hunk, hump	WALKER	A walker, the Phantom
JACKSON	Michael, car jack	WANG	Wham
JAMES	Jams	WASHINGTON	Washing machine
JOHNSON	Toilet (the John)	WATSON	Wet suit
JONES	Jokes, cones	WEST	Wild west, vest
KELLY	Gallery, Ned Kelly	WHITE	Wide
KENNEDY	Can of Tea	WILLIAMS	A will with arms
KING	King	WILSON	Whistle
KRAMER	Creamer	WOODS	Woods, warts
LAU	Loud	ZAMMIT	Summit

Summary

Technique 1. How to Give Sincere Compliments
- Compliment a person's behaviour, appearance or possessions.
- Say *what* you like and tell them *why* you like it.
- Begin with the person's name
- If someone compliments you, accept it, thank them and explain why you're grateful for the compliment.

Technique 2. How to Listen Effectively
- Use 'active listening'. Paraphrase what the person said and feed it back to them, starting with the word 'you'.
- Don't interrupt the speaker.
- Stick to the subject.
- Let them finish what they're saying.
- Use Minimal Encouragers.

Technique 3. How to say 'Thank You'
- Say your thanks clearly and distinctly.
- Look at and touch the person you're thanking.
- Use the person's name.
- Send a written thank you note

Technique 4. How to Remember Peoples' Names
- Repeat the name
- Turn their name into an object
- Imagine the object interacting in a ridiculous situation with their most prominent feature

SECTION B

How to Be a Great Conversationalist

5

How to Talk with People (and be extremely interesting)

People who are perceived as interesting, talk about the other person's favourite subject – themselves. There are three ways to do this:

1. Be interested in others and encourage them to talk about themselves and their interests.

A person is more sincerely interested in the pimple on their nose than how many AIDS sufferers there are in Africa. You'll make more friends in 4 weeks being interested in others than you will in ten years of trying to get others to be interested in you.

2. Remove the words 'I, Me and Mine' from your vocabulary and replace them with 'You' and 'Yours'.

Instead of saying:

'**I** know how successful this plan is because **my** other clients tell **me** how **my** advice has helped achieve what they told **me** they wanted.'

Say:

> 'When **you** take this action **you'll** be excited about the results **you'll** achieve because it will benefit **you** and **your** family in ways **you** couldn't have imagined.'

3. Ask only questions that get them to talk about themselves

> "How was **your** holiday?"
> "How did **you** get started in **your** line of work?"
> "How's **your** son going at his new school?"
> "Who do **you** believe will win the next election?"
> "What do **you** think about (whatever)?"

The Bottom Line – people are not interested in you or me – they are only interested in *themselves*. If you feel upset about this – get over it. Accept it as a fact of life.

6

How to Ask Great Questions

Most conversations have difficulty starting or continuing, not because of the things being discussed, but because the wrong type of questions are being used.

There are two types of questions you can ask:

1. Closed-Ended Questions

Closed-Ended questions ask for only a one or two word answer and make the conversation stop. For example,

Q: "When did you start work as an accountant?"
A: "8 years ago."
Q: "Did you like the movie?"
A: "Yes."
Q: "Who do you think will win the election?"
A: "The Liberals."

Closed questions make the conversation sound like an interrogation.

2. Open-Ended Questions

Open-Ended questions ask for explanations, opinions and elaborations and quickly build rapport with people because they show others

that you're interested in them and what they have to say. People who ask Open-Ended questions are perceived as being interesting, sincere, dynamic and caring.

The four most powerful Open-Ended questions you can ask begin with:

How...?
Tell me about...
In what way...?
Why...?

Here are the same questions asked in an Open-Ended form:

Q: "**How** did you get started as an accountant?"
A: "When I was in school I was always interested in how numbers could influence outcomes... etc, etc."
Q: "**Tell me about** the part of the movie you enjoyed most?"
A: "I loved the scene where Dracula came through the door and said... etc, etc."
Q: "**In what way** do you feel the Labor candidate has influenced this election?"
A: "I've never voted for the Conservatives but I think that last night's debate could be the deciding factor because...etc, etc."

Practice asking only Open-Ended questions. If you ask a Closed-Ended question, immediately follow through with an Open-Ended one.

For example:

Q: "When did you move to Chesterville?" (Closed)
A: "About 10 years ago."
Q: "**Why** do you think Chesterville has changed so much in that time?" (Open)
A: "Well, when we first moved here there was not much development happening but five years ago the developers moved in and... etc."

7

How to Start a Conversation

People form up to 90% of their opinion about you in the first four minutes of meeting you so it's critical to have effective ways to start conversations in any situation. You have only three opening topics to choose from to start the conversation:

- the situation
- the other person
- yourself

and only three ways to begin:

- asking a question
- giving an opinion
- stating a fact

1. Talking about the Situation

Talking about the situation you are both in is usually the simplest and easiest way to start. Simply look around and ask an Open-Ended question about what you notice. This can be done anywhere, for example -

At a market: "I notice you're buying zucchinis. I've never known how to cook them. How do you prepare them?"

At an art gallery: "What do you think the artist was trying to say?"

At a meeting: "How did you happen to be at this meeting?"

In a line at a restaurant: "Why do you think this place is so popular?"

In a supermarket: "What do you think is the best way to use this detergent?"

Opening a business presentation: "How did you get started in this line of business?"

2. Talking about the Other Person

People love to talk about themselves and are happy to respond to any questions you ask about them.

At a party: "That's an interesting emblem on your jacket. What does it stand for?"

At a golf course: "You've got a great swing. How did you perfect it?"

At a meeting: "I notice you voted for redevelopment of the park. In what way do you think the park could be improved?"

At the beach: "I see you belong to the Lifesaving club. How does someone get started in that?"

3. Talking About Yourself

The rule here is simple – unless someone asks you a question about yourself, your family, your possessions or your occupation, they're simply *not* interested. When starting a conversation, never volunteer information about yourself unless someone asks.

How to Keep a Conversation Going

Use Bridges

People who give short answers to Open-Ended questions are best handled with a 'bridge' to keep them talking. Bridges in effect, are shortened versions of Open-Ended questions. They are best used with people who give brief answers to Open-Ended questions.

Bridges include:

Meaning..?
For example..?
So then..?
Therefore..?
Then you..?
Which means..?

The use of a bridge must be followed by silence on your part.

John: "How did you happen to move to this area?"
Martin: "I like the climate better."
John: *"Better than...?"*
Martin: "...better than the polluted air in the city."

John: *"Which means...?"*

Martin: "...which means improved health for me and my family. In fact, I read a report the other day that said people's overall health was deteriorating and ... etc."

In this example, John used two bridges; he has the ball rolling and doesn't sound like an interrogator. And he's not doing most of the talking.

You need to use two physical actions to use a bridge successfully:

1. Lean forward with your palm out when you say the bridge
2. Lean back and stop talking after using the bridge

Leaning forward with your palm out conveys that you are non-threatening and lets the listener know that it's his turn to talk by 'handing over' the control.

When you've used a bridge, *stop talking!* Resist the urge to add pearls of wisdom to the seemingly endless silence that can sometimes follow the use of a bridge. The outstretched palm gives the responsibility to speak next to the listener, so let him come up with the next statement. After you have given the control, lean back or sit back, put your hand on your chin and nod your head. This encourages the listener to keep talking.

Bridges are fun to use; they make conversations more productive and give you the power of silent control. When bridges are combined with Minimal Encouragers, they become some of the most dynamic tools you have in your bag to keep conversations going.

9

How to Keep Others Interested in your Conversations

Who makes more friends than anyone and is always accepted by every person he meets? The answer is – a dog. As soon as he sees you he wags his tail with excitement, thinks you're perfect in every way and is only interested in you and you alone. He never has a negative word to say about you, thinks you're a great singer and the later at night you come home, the more excited he is to see you.

He gives you unconditional love with no ulterior motives, no demands for compensation and doesn't want you to buy life insurance from him.

Only talk to people about the things that interest *them*, not the things that interest you. Most people only care about what *they* want and are interested in, and not in what you want.

You see, if you go fishing, there's no point in baiting your hook with something *you* like to eat like steak, hamburgers or chocolate ice-cream. Put something on the hook that the *fish* loves – a worm or a smelly prawn. This is the only way to influence others. Talk only in terms of what *they* want.

Most people are not effective or interesting when they talk with others because they only talk about *themselves* and their own needs.

You can only capture others' attention by discussing what *they* want and showing them *how* to get it.

10

How to Make People Feel Instantly Positive About You

Whatever facial expressions you send to others, they will send them straight back to you. Evidence shows that responding positively to a smiling face is hardwired into the brain. A smile communicates "I'm happy to see you and I accept you". This is why everyone loves constant smilers, like babies.

Professor Ruth Campbell, from University College, London, discovered a 'mirror neuron' in the brain which triggers the part responsible for the recognition of faces and expressions and causes an instant mirroring reaction. In other words, whether we realize it or not, we automatically copy the expressions we see.

In humans, smiling serves much the same purpose as it does with other primates. It shows another person you are non-threatening and asks them to accept you on a personal level. This response is also hardwired into the brain.

This is why smiling regularly is such an important habit to develop as a part of your body language repertoire, even when you don't feel like smiling, because it directly influences other people's attitudes to you and how they respond to you.

Frowning is a negative facial expression to have when talking with others because they perceive that you either don't like them

or are critical of them. If you are a frowner, try putting your hand on your forehead when you talk, to train yourself out of this destructive habit.

Summary

When you smile at another person they will almost always return your smile. This causes positive feelings in you both because of cause and effect. Studies show that most encounters will run smoother, last longer, have more positive outcomes and dramatically improve relationships when you make a point of regularly smiling and laughing often. Practice this to the point where smiling becomes a habit.

Evidence also shows that smiles and laughter build your immune system, defend against illness and disease, medicate the body, sell ideas, attract more friends and extend life.

Humor heals.

Smile!

11

How to Empathize with People

Most people want others to empathize with them or their cause, and to feel understood. The FEEL-FELT-FOUND technique achieves this goal and makes people feel positive toward you. Rather than disagreeing with a complaint or grievance, you say:

"I understand how you FEEL. I know someone who was in a similar situation to you and they FELT the same way. They FOUND that by (give your solution) they were able to reach a positive outcome."

If someone said:

'I can't do business with your organization because I hear your service is lousy',

you'd respond:

'I understand exactly how you FEEL. One of our long-standing and valued customers FELT exactly the same way. But, they FOUND that simply by placing their order before noon they received same day delivery.'

If Sue said:

'I don't think I love you Justin'

He could say:

'I know how you **FEEL** Sue. Jessica once **FELT** the same way about Paul, but when they sat down and discussed their situation, she **FOUND** that, deep down, Paul was really a caring, sharing guy.'

In both of these cases, you have not disagreed with the other person or argued the point. In fact, you almost sound as if you've agreed with them. Don't defend an attack from someone; acknowledge their feelings.

How to be Agreeable with *Everyone* (even those who criticize you)

Having an agreeable manner is one of the most important habits you can cultivate. People love those who are agreeable and dislike those who disagree. To be agreeable with anyone who is critical of you, either agree if it's true or agree with the critic's right to their opinion.

1. How to agree with the Truth

The most powerful response you can give to your critic is to agree with the truth of what they say and then restate your position.
  For example:

Mother: If you go dancing tonight, you'll have trouble getting out of bed for work in the morning.
Daughter: You're probably right! But I love dancing and can't wait to go!

The daughter has *agreed with the truth* of her mother's criticism, while at the same time maintaining her own position.

> **Sue:** I don't think you should quit your job, Adam. You're a key person in the company and if the economy goes bad you'll still have a job. Going into business alone has no guarantees!
>
> **Adam:** You're absolutely right, Sue. There are no guarantees but I know I'll do well and I'm really looking forward to this opportunity!

Adam agreed with the truth of what Sue said. He didn't argue with her or put himself or her down and he still maintained his position without being aggressive.

2. How to agree with your critic's right to an opinion

Often, you will disagree with your critic's opinion, but you can still agree with their right to have an opinion, however silly you think their opinion is.

For example:

> **David:** If you keep on spending all your money on clothes Monica, you'll end up broke!
>
> **Monica:** I understand how you might feel that way Dave, but I just love the feeling of having a lot of different outfits.

> **Leanne:** How could you buy a Mazda, Glen? You know Toyotas are much better cars!
>
> **Glen:** Your opinion is understandable, Leanne and – you're right – Toyotas are great cars, but I just love the feel of the Mazda!

Glen and Monica both agreed with their critic's right to an opinion – Glen also agreed with the truth – but neither backed away from their position or made the other person feel wrong. Even when you <u>totally</u> disagree with their criticism, there is usually a way of being agreeable while affirming what you believe to be the truth. You're goal should be to always make others feel right, even when you don't agree with them.

Here are the five keys to becoming an agreeable person:

1. **Decide to be agreeable with every person you meet.**
   Develop an agreeable nature and make others feel right.

2. **Agree with the Truth.**
   Let others know that you agree with something they said. Nod your head and say, 'Yes, you're right' or 'I agree with you'.

3. **Agree with your critic's right to an opinion.**
   Even when you think they are talking complete nonsense, acknowledge that it's OK for them to think that way while, at the same time, you restate what you believe to be true.

4. **Admit it when you are wrong.**
   People who admit fault are admired by others but most people prefer to deny, lie or lay blame.. If you're wrong say:

   'I certainly got that wrong...'
   'I really blew it ...'
   'I was wrong ...'

5. **Avoid arguing.**
   You can rarely win an argument, even if you're right. Arguing loses friends and credibility and gives fighters what they want – a fight.

13

How to Create Positive 'Vibes' About Yourself

People form up to 90% of their first opinion about us in under four minutes and their initial evaluations of us are based primarily on our Body Language. Next, they listen to how we speak and what we say, then they determine their level of respect for us and their interest in us.

To command other's admiration and respect early in an initial meeting, do the following three things:

1. Be positive of who you are and what you do

Talk in glowing terms about your station in life and why you like it. Never put yourself down by saying things like, 'I'm just a clerk, only a housewife, etc.' Instead say, 'I work for the country's biggest bank helping people realise their investment goals' or, 'I'm the mother to two beautiful children and a life partner to John'.

If you can't be positive about who you are, neither can anyone else.

2. Be Enthusiastic

Talk about life with positive expectancy. Not only will this sell you to others, they'll also become enthusiastic about you and your conversations. Always smile – it makes people wonder what you've been up to.

3. Don't criticize anyone or anything

When you criticize, it is decoded by others as low self-esteem, lack of understanding or your lack of self-confidence. If someone mentions a competitor, praise the competitor's good points. If you can't say something positive, don't say anything. Don't try to build yourself up by knocking someone else down.

14

How to Make it Easy for People to say 'Yes'

Here are four ways to help a person say 'yes' to your proposal –

1. Find a reason for them to say 'yes'

Everything we do and any course of action we choose in life is motivated by a specific reason. Sometimes there are several reasons for doing something but there is always one dominant reason and this is what you need to uncover. By asking, 'What is your number one priority?' and listening to the answer without interruption, the other person will give you the reasons why they would be motivated to take action. Never assume you know a person's main reason for doing something, because you may be wrong and they won't feel motivated to take action. Never give a person *your* personal reasons for doing something unless your reasons are identical to theirs. When you uncover what *they* want, show them how they can get it using *your* solution. People are more persuaded toward the things they discover themselves rather than you telling them about it. Let them work out their problems themselves. All you need to do is ask the right questions that lead them to the right conclusion. As you explain your solution, replay the exact words *they* said about their number one priority.

2. Ask only 'yes' questions.

Open conversations by asking questions that can only be answered with a 'yes'. Avoid questions that will result in a 'no' answer.

Here are some examples of 'yes' questions:

'Are you interested in making money?'
'Would I be right in saying you want your family to be happy?'
'Would you like to spend more time with your children?'

Make their meeting with you a positive 'yes' experience and they will find it difficult to say 'no' to you later on. When influencing others, remember that your objective is to prove them right, not wrong – even if you don't agree with their point of view.

3. Nod your head

When we feel positive, we nod our heads. Research shows that if you *intentionally* nod your head, you'll experience positive feelings. Nod your head as you ask your 'yes' questions or as you listen to their responses, and watch how others *also* begin to nod their head and start to feel positive about your proposals.

4. Offer them a choice between two 'yeses'

When you offer only one option, the other person is forced to decide between 'yes' and 'no' – and 'no' is usually the option chosen by most people because it's safe. Offer a choice between two things you want them to do.

For example:

'Would it be better to meet you at 3pm or would 4pm be better?'
'Do you like the green – or is the blue better?'
'Will you use a credit card or would cash be more suitable?'
'When will you start – Wednesday or Thursday?'

How to Talk so Men will Listen

Research has shown that men use a specialized set of rules for communication with each other. If you are female, it's very important to understand these rules and abide by them when dealing with any male.

Here are the rules of 'Manspeak', formulated from the results of brain scans that track the blood flow and function of the male brain:

1. Give a man one thing at a time

Men's brains are compartmentalized. It's as if a man's brain is divided into little rooms with each room containing a function that works in isolation of all others. Do not multi-track with a man. Keep your ideas and thoughts separated. Deal with one thing at a time.

2. Let him have his turn to speak

Male brains are wired to either speak or listen. Most men can't do both simultaneously and this is why men take turns to talk. Let him have his turn and let him finish his sentence. Do not interrupt.

3. Use a poker face when listening

Men think that someone who uses many facial expressions when listening may have mental or emotional problems. Hold a serious expression when listening to a man and make listening sounds like, 'uh-huh…', 'I see…', 'hmmm…', 'Yeah, yeah…' to encourage him to continue.

4. Give him facts and information

Male brains are organized for spatial tasks and are interested in the relationship between things. Show solutions to problems, give facts and testimonials. Avoid emotional pleas. Instead, prove your point.

5. Use direct speech

Men's sentences are shorter than women's and contain more facts, data, information and solutions. Don't hint or infer things. Say what you mean and get to the point.

16

How to Talk so Women will Listen

Research has shown that women have a specialized set of rules for communication with each other. If you are male, it's vital that you understand these rules and comply with them when dealing with any female.

Here are the rules of 'Womanspeak', formulated from the results of brain scans that track the blood flow in the female brain:

1. Participate in the conversation

Don't wait for your turn to talk. Female brains are wired to both speak *and* listen simultaneously, which is why women often seem to all talk at the same time. This is because they <u>can</u>. If you wait for your turn you'll just get older. If you don't actively participate in a conversation with women, it is perceived as a lack of interest by you or that you hold a critical opinion.

2. Use facial expressions when listening

A woman's facial expressions reveal her emotions so, as she talks, mirror her expressions and gestures to create rapport. Never do this with another man.

3. Give her personal details and appeal to her emotions

Female brains are organized for reading the emotions of others and for evaluating relationships between people. Reveal to her, personal information about yourself and your family and volunteer your personal feelings about things.

4. Use indirect speech

Women's spoken sentences are longer than men's and may contain several subjects including her feelings and emotions about those subjects. Avoid getting to the point quickly, pushing for a fast solution to a problem, or 'closing the sale'. Be more friendly, relaxed and agreeable.

17

The 17 Powerless Phrases you Must Remove from Your Vocabulary

This is a list of some of the most damaging words and phrases you can speak. These phrases appear to say one thing while they in fact reveal the emotions, feeling and prejudices of the speaker. Eliminate them from your own vocabulary because they detract from your credibility.

What is said	What is heard
Kind of… Sort of thing…	You're not confident or don't know what you're talking about
You know what I mean…	You're unsure of what you're saying
The wife/husband/partner	Depersonalization of your partner
Truthfully Frankly Honestly Sincerely Believe me	People who are about to be dishonest, insincere, exaggerate or tell a lie often begin sentences with these words
Of course	You're trying to force agreement
Should/Ought	You're trying to force agreement through guilt or a sense of duty
Don't get me wrong	You're about to say something negative or critical

What is said	What is Heard
In my humble opinion…	You're about to make an egotistical statement
I don't want to be…	That's what you really want to be; e.g 'I don't want to be rude' is followed by a rude statement
I'll try	I don't expect to succeed
I'll do my best	My best isn't good enough
With respect	I have no respect for you

Be aware of these powerless words and phrases and make a point of eliminating them from your vocabulary.

The 12 Most Powerful Words You Can Use

A study at the University of California showed the most persuasive words in spoken language are:

discovery, guarantee, love, proven, results, save, easy, health, money, new, safety, you.

The new results you'll get from the discovery of these proven words will guarantee you more love, better health and will save you money. They're completely safe, and easy to use.

Practice these words and make them a normal part of your everyday conversations.

19

Turn Negative Statements into Positives

You can almost always find a way to turn destructive criticism into constructive praise. Instead of criticizing others for failing, you can compliment them for trying or for improving in some small way. Consider these examples:

Instead of saying...	You could say...
Too bad you didn't get the pay rise	Barbara, I think it's great that you told your boss what you want, even if you didn't get it. What do you suppose you can do next to change his mind?
That story you wrote is ridiculous	Valerie, I like the paragraph where Burt is being forced to either marry or walk the plank because the words you used make it come alive for me. Where did you get the idea for that scene?
It took you five attempts to pass the test? What was the problem?	You stuck it out, Bill. Not everyone could have done that. What are you doing to celebrate?
You bombed out again! Guess you'll have to wait a few more months before you can start again.	Congratulations, Sue. You walked a step further than you did yesterday!

How to Deal with Fear and Worry

Studies have shown that of all the things we worry about in life:

> 87% never happen
> 7% actually occur
> 6% you will have some influence over the outcome

This means that most things in life that you worry about won't happen and that you have little to no control over the few things that do happen. So it doesn't pay to worry about the things you fear.

Approach fear for what it really is –

False
Evidence
Appearing
Real

Fear is nothing more than a physical reaction to thinking about the consequences you don't want. Most of your worries will never come to pass anyway, so they are nothing more than

False Evidence Appearing Real.

Never think about what you *don't* want to happen. Only think about what you *do* want, regardless of the outcome of a situation. What you think about is what you'll usually get.

Summary

Technique 5. How to Talk with People
- People are primarily interested in *themselves*.
- Remove the words 'I, Me and Mine' from your vocabulary and replace them with 'You' and 'Yours'.

Technique 6. How to Ask Great Questions
- Ask Open-Ended questions. Begin with: 'How?', 'Why?', 'In what way?', 'Tell me about…'

Technique 7. How to Start a Conversation
- Start the conversation by talking about either the situation or the other person
- Open with a question.

Technique 8. How to Keep a Conversation Going
- Use bridges such as: 'For example?', 'So then...?', 'Therefore?', 'Then you…?', 'Which means…?'

Technique 9. How to keep Others Interested in your Conversations
- Discuss only what *they* want and show them *how* to get it using your solutions.

Technique 10. How to Make People Feel Instantly Positive about You
- Smile at everyone. A smile communicates "I'm happy to see you and I accept you".

Technique 11. How to Empathize with People

- Tell others you know how they FEEL and that others have FELT the same way. Then explain the solutions they FOUND.

Technique 12. How to be Agreeable with *Everyone*

- Agree with the Truth of a criticism.
- Agree with the critic's right to an opinion.

Technique 13. How to Create Positive 'Vibes' about Yourself.

- Be positive of who you are and what you do.
- Be enthusiastic when you speak.
- Don't criticize anyone or anything.

Technique 14. How to Make it Easy for People to say 'Yes'

- Find a reason for them to say 'yes'.
- Ask only 'yes' questions.
- Nod your head when speaking and listening.
- Offer a choice between two 'yeses'

Technique 15. How to Talk so Men will Listen

- Give a man one thing at a time.
- Give facts and information.
- Let him have his turn to speak.
- Hold a poker face and use listening sounds when listening.
- Use direct speech.

Technique 16. How to Talk so Women will Listen
- Participate in the conversation. Don't wait for your turn.
- Use facial expressions while listening.
- Give personal details and appeal to her emotions.
- Don't push too early for solutions or conclusions.
- Use Indirect Talk. Don't be pushy.

Technique 17. The 17 Powerless Phrases to Remove
- Remove phrases and words that detract from your credibility, including – Kind of, Sort of thing, You know what I mean, The wife/husband/partner, Truthfully, Honestly, Frankly, Sincerely, Believe me, Of course, Should, Ought, Don't get me wrong, In my humble opinion, I don't want to be , I'll try, I'll do my best, With respect.

Technique 18. The 12 Most Powerful Words to Use
- The 12 most important words you can use are – discovery, guarantee, love, proven, results, save, easy, health, money, new, safety, you.

Technique 19. Turn Negative Statements into Positives
- Find a way to turn destructive criticisms into constructive praise.

Technique 20. How to Deal with Fear and Worry
- Almost everything you worry about won't happen and you have little control over the few things that will. So don't worry about everything.
- Approach fear for what it mostly is – **F**alse **E**vidence **A**ppearing **R**eal.

SECTION C

Giving Business Presentations

21

How to Make Lasting First Impressions

First impressions are the 'love-at-first-sight' of the business world. Here are the Nine Golden Opening Moves:

1. **Your Entry:** When you are invited to enter a room, walk in without hesitation. Do not stand in the doorway like a naughty schoolchild waiting to see the headmaster. People who lack confidence change gears and perform a small shuffle as they enter a room. Walk through the door with purpose and maintain the same speed.

2. **Your Approach:** Walk briskly. Influential people and those who command attention walk briskly at a medium pace with medium length strides. People who walk slowly or take long strides convey that they have plenty of time on their hands, are not interested in what they are doing or have nothing else to do.

3. **The Handshake:** Keep your palm straight (vertical) and return the grip pressure you receive. Let the other person decide when to end the handshake. Never shake hands directly across a desk as it can leave the other person having the 'Upper Hand' over you.

4. **Your Smile:** Make sure your teeth are visible when you smile, and smile with your whole face, not just your mouth.

5. **The Eyebrow Flash:** This is an ancient acknowledgement signal that is hardwired into the brain to be sent and received by others. Simply raise your eyebrows for a split second as you acknowledge the person.

6. **When you talk:** Use a person's name twice in the first 15 seconds and never talk for more than 30 seconds at a time. Speak at a slightly slower pace than they speak.

7. **When you sit:** If you are compelled to sit in a low chair directly facing the other person, turn away to an angle of 45 degrees to the person to avoid being caught in the 'reprimand' position. If you can't angle your chair, angle your body away.

8. **Your Gestures:** People who are cool, calm and in control of their emotions use clear, uncomplicated, deliberate movements. High status individuals use fewer gestures than low status individuals. Don't raise your hands higher than your chin. To create rapport, mirror the other person's gestures and expressions when appropriate.

9. **Your Exit:** When you're finished, pack your things calmly and deliberately – not in a frenzy – shake hands if possible, turn and walk out. If the door was closed when you entered, close it behind you as you leave. People watch you from behind as you leave so if you're a man, make sure the back of your shoes are shined. Hidden cameras show that, if you're a woman, others study your rear as you depart – whether you like it or not. When you get to the door, turn around slowly and smile. It's better that they recall your smiling face than your rear end.

22

How to Handle Criticism in Business

If a client or potential customer criticizes you or your organization, use the 'Put the Boot on His Foot' technique to diffuse the situation. Simply ask the person what *they* would do if they were in your situation and someone gave *them* the same criticism.

Whatever they say, you respond with:

> "That's right! That's what we did!" or, "You're right! And that's what we're going to do!"

For example:

> **Prospect:** "I've heard your delivery time is poor."
> **You:** "Yes, it's true that we had some problems at our warehouse at one stage. Tell me, if you were the manager of a company that received that criticism, what would you do?"
> **Prospect:** "I'd call a meeting of everyone concerned and work out a solid plan that would *guarantee* deliveries were made on time!"
> **You:** You're absolutely right! And that's exactly what we did."

You have *agreed with the truth* and made your prospect feel right by stating that, not only is his opinion correct, your company has already taken it on board (or intends to take it). When you 'Put the Boot on His Foot', your prospect's objection becomes deflated and he won't feel the urge to raise it again.

If your company hasn't made the necessary changes to fix the problem then you don't deserve the prospect's business.

The Most Commanding Way to Answer the Telephone

Most people answer the telephone like this:

"XYZ Corporation... Allan speaking."

If you were walking toward someone, you wouldn't say "I'm Allan, walking.' On the phone it's obvious to the caller that you're speaking so don't say the word *'speaking'*.

Research shows that a person will recall the last word they hear when you answer the phone, so say your **name** last and use a Rising Terminal. A Rising Terminal is where you raise the volume and inflection of your voice. Studies show that when you do this, 86% of callers can recall your name versus 6% who can recall it when you answer with 'Allan *speaking...*'

From today, answer the telephone:

"XYZ Corporation... This is Allan."

and use a Rising Terminal on your name. This also prompts the caller to give you their name and a relationship can be immediately established. By the way, use *your* name, not Allan's.

How to Give a Reprimand or Critique

There are times when you, as a leader, will need to bring someone to account or point out behaviors that are unacceptable or non-productive. Most of us dread the thought of giving someone corrective action or discipline. The following 6-part technique can make it quick, powerful and painless for all concerned.

The 6 Golden Rules for a successful critique, reprimand or appraisal

1. Use the 'Sandwich Technique'

Onions taste bitter when eaten alone but can taste good when mixed with other salad items. To soften the blow, praise the person for something positive that he has done. Then deliver the criticism followed by another positive point about his performance.

2. Criticize the act, not the person

Explain that you are happy with him personally (assuming that's true!) but not with what he did.

3. Ask for their help

Never demand that a person 'does as they're told'. Say you need their co-operation and help to solve a problem.

4. Admit that you've made similar mistakes, and give the answer

Begin a criticism by talking about a similar mistake you've made in the past. This makes your criticism more digestible, just like a dentist giving anesthetic before drilling a person's teeth. Explain that you (and others) have had similar challenges to deal with in the past and show how you fixed the problem. When you admit that you are not perfect, others are influenced to follow your lead.

5. Make the criticism once, and do it in private

Never reprimand a person in front of others. Do it behind closed doors in a calm way and only mention the offence and its solution once. Do not keep hammering away about the person's poor performance.

6. End on a friendly note

Thank them for their co-operation in solving the problem and say that you look forward to seeing them deal with things in the new ways you have both discussed.

25

How to Give a Persuasive Speech

People who can stand and give a powerful, motivational talk are admired by everyone and are promoted into leadership positions both in business and socially.

Here is a four-step formula for giving a motivational speech 'off the top of your head' on any topic, whether it's for two minutes, twenty minutes or an hour. Memorize the following four points:

1. Ho-Hum
2. Why bring that up?
3. For example?
4. So what?

1. Ho-Hum

When you first stand to speak, the audience is silently thinking, 'Ho-hum… another dull speaker' so you must open with a dramatic, riveting or humorous story, statement or line that jolts the audience out of their complacency and grabs their attention.

2. Why bring that up?

Your next step is to tell them why you made the dramatic/humorous/ riveting statement or story and why it is important to them.

3. For example?

This is where most of the body of your talk will be. Give three points or reasons about why what you're saying is true and important to them. When giving a longer talk, give three supporting points for each of your main three points.

4. So what?

At the end of your speech, your audience may be thinking, 'So, what do you want me to do about it?' and this is where you motivate them to embrace the ideas, thoughts or course of action you're suggesting.

Let's say, for example, you've been asked to talk to a group of parents about road safety and your objective is to convince them to use the pedestrian crossing and not walk randomly with their children across the busy road. Here's how you'd deliver it:

1. Ho-Hum

"Two thousand, three hundred and fifty-five children were needlessly crippled or had their lives cut short last year – and their parents are to blame. Statistically, two of you in this room will soon be looking into the eyes of a hospitalized child and praying that things will be alright. The question is – who of you will it be?"

2. Why bring that up?

"I bring up these statistics, ladies and gentlemen, because that's how many children were hit by cars in this country last year while crossing the road to meet their parents. And 96% of these children were not on a pedestrian crossing. What I am about to say is critical to each of you in this room. And that's because you love your children."

3. For Example?

(*Point 1*) "The National Safety Council conducted a study outside 46 schools recently and discovered ..." (back up your first point by quoting facts, statistics and other data).

(*Point 2*) "We conducted our own survey of parent's attitudes to road safety in our own neighborhood and found ..." (prove your second point).

(*Point 3*) "As a parent myself – and I know most of you have felt this same way – I have asked myself many times ..." (your third point, perhaps involving a personal, emotional opinion).

4. So what?

"So here's what I want you to do. From today, the next time you pick up your child from school, I want you to ..." (motivate your audience to do what you suggest).

When you've finished your talk, shut up and sit down.

Never thank the audience for listening to you – if you've done a good job, they should be thanking you.

How to Use a Visual Presentation

Research shows that when you are giving a visual presentation using books, charts, graphs or a laptop, 82% of the information is absorbed via the eyes, 11% via the ears, and 7% through the other senses.

Tell, show and involve

The Wharton study in the United States found that the retention of information from verbal presentations was only 10%. By comparison, the retention rate of a combined verbal and visual presentation is 51%. This means you can achieve a 400% increase in efficiency with the use of visual presentation aids.

The study also found using a visual aid can cut the average business meeting time from 25.7 minutes to 18.6 minutes – a 28% time saving.

But when however, we present our story using verbal, visual and emotional involvement, a person's retention rate rises to 92%.

We retain:

> 10% of what we hear
> 51% of what we see <u>and</u> hear
> 92% of what we see <u>and</u> hear <u>and</u> become involved in

So, when you only say it, it has the least effect. Telling *and* showing has a moderate effect. Telling, showing and getting others involved as you present gives the maximum retention.

Use the Power Lift

Use a pen to point to your presentation while at the same time, verbalise what the other person sees. Next, raise the pen from the presentation and hold it between his eyes and your eyes. This is called the *Power Lift* and has the magnetic effect of lifting his head so that he is looking directly at you and can *see* and *hear* what you are saying. This helps achieve a higher absorption of your message than from just talking. Keep the palm of your other hand visible when you are speaking.

Hold stronger eye contact with men when presenting your story but less frequently with women. If you're uncertain, mirror the amount of eye contact the other person gives you.

27

How to Decide Where to Sit in an Interview

Certain strategies using chairs and seating arrangements can create both persuasive or negative moods in an office or home.

There are five positions you can take at a rectangular table. Assume you are person A and the other person is B.

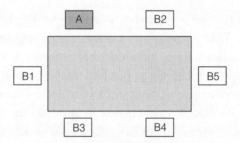

The Competitive/Defensive Position (B3)

The table is a solid barrier between both parties. Sitting across from a person can create a defensive, competitive environment and can lead to each party taking a firm stand on his own point of view.

Research into business encounters found that 56% of people perceive this position as competitive. In a business setting, this position is taken by people who are either competing with each

other or if one is reprimanding the other. People who sit opposite speak less, are more negative, competitive or aggressive. If you are compelled to sit here, angle your chair to 45 degrees away from person A.

The Co-operative Position (B2)

When two people are thinking alike or both working on a task together, this position often occurs. The studies found that 55% of people chose this position as the most co-operative place to sit or intuitively sat there when asked to work jointly with another person. It is one of the best positions for presenting your story and having it accepted. It also allows for good eye contact and the opportunity for mirroring the other person's body language.

The Corner Position (B1)

This position is used by people who are engaged in friendly, casual conversation. This is the most strategic position from which you can deliver a presentation, assuming that person A is the audience. By simply moving the chair to position B1 you can relieve a tense atmosphere and increase the chances of a positive outcome.

Positions B4 and B5 are chosen in a library to communicate independence or non-involvement and should be avoided for giving presentations.

If you're invited to sit in an informal area of a person's office or home, such as at a round coffee table, it's a positive signal because 95% of business rejections are delivered from *behind* a desk. Never sit in a low sofa that sinks so low it makes you look like a giant pair of legs topped by a small head. If necessary, sit upright on the edge of the chair so you can control your body language, and angle your body to 45 degrees away from the person.

28

Ten Winning Body Language Strategies That Give You the Edge

As we've stated, people form up to 90% of their opinion about you in under 4 minutes and 60% – 80% of the impact you will make on them is non-verbal. The following ten strategies will give you the best opportunity to make a positive effect on others.

1. Keep Your Palms Up

Keep your palms visible when you talk. The response to this ancient signal is hard-wired into the brain. They will read you as non-threatening and will respond positively to you.

2. Keep Your Fingers Together

People who keep their fingers closed and their hands below their chin when they talk command the most attention. Using open fingers or having your hands held above the chin is perceived as less authoritative.

3. Keep Your Elbows Out

Sitting with your elbows on the armrest of a chair is perceived as a position of power and conveys a strong, upright image. Humble, defeated individuals let their arms drop inside the arms of the chair and they keep their elbows close to their bodies to protect themselves. They are perceived as fearful or negative, so avoid sitting like this.

4. Keep Your Distance

Respect the person's personal space, which will be greatest in the opening minutes of a new meeting. If you move in too close, the person may respond by sitting back, leaning away or using gestures that reveal their irritation, such as drumming their fingers or clicking a pen. Sit closer to familiar people but further back from new ones. Sit closer to those of similar age and further back from significantly older or younger ones.

5. Mirror Their Body Language

Mirroring the other person's body language and speech patterns builds rapport quickly. In a new meeting with someone, mirror his sitting position, posture, body angle, gestures, facial expressions and tone of voice. Before long, they'll start to feel that there's something about you they like – they'll describe you as easy to be with.

When presenting to couples, watch for who mirrors whom to uncover the decision-maker. If the woman makes the initial movements and the man copies, there is little point in asking him for a decision.

6. Match Their Speech Rate

A person's speed of speaking reveals the rate at which their brain can analyze information. Speak at the same rate or slightly slower than the other person and mirror their inflection and intonation. Studies show that others describe feeling 'pressured' when someone speaks faster than they do.

7. Uncross All Arms

Arms folded across the chest is an attempt to put a barrier between the person and something they don't like. A person's recall of what was said decreases by up to 40% when they fold their arms. Change someone's folded-arms position by handing them something to hold or giving them something to do. Give them a pen, book, brochure, sample or written test to encourage them to unfold their arms and lean forward. To be persuasive, *never* cross your own arms in any face to face meeting.

8. Touch Their Elbow

Mirror the touch you receive. If they don't touch you, leave them alone. Experiments however, have found that when a person is touched lightly on the elbow for not longer than three seconds, they are 68% more likely to be co-operative than if they weren't touched at all.

Studies show that female waitresses who were taught to touch the elbows and hands of their dining customers made 80% more tips from male diners than the non-touching waitresses, while male waiters increased their earnings by 32% regardless of which sex they touched. In other words, skilful elbow and hand touching can give you up to three times the chance of getting what you want.

9. Repeat Their Name

When you next meet someone new and you shake hands, extend your left arm, give a light touch on their elbow or hand as you shake and repeat their name to confirm you heard it correctly. Not only does this make the person feel important, it lets you remember their name through the repetition.

10. Avoid Touching Your Face

Studies show that when someone is concealing information or lying, their nose and face touching increases dramatically due to an increase in blood pressure when lying. Even if you have an itchy nose, people who don't know you may think you're lying. So keep your hands away from your face.

Practice It All

Before you go to an important interview or meeting, sit quietly for a few minutes and mentally rehearse the abovementioned things, seeing yourself doing them well. When your mind can see them clearly, your body will be able to carry them out. You need to cast yourself into a believable role in an interview, so practice mentally, in advance, how you will act, if you want others to take you seriously.

Evidence shows that, with practice, these skills will soon become second nature to you and serve you well for the rest of your life.

Summary

Technique 21. How to make Lasting First Impressions
- When you enter a room, walk in briskly, without hesitation.
- Keep your handshake vertical and return the grip you receive.
- Smile. Show your teeth and smile with your whole face.
- Raise your eyebrows for a split second.
- Use the person's name twice in the first 15 seconds.
- Angle your body to 45 degrees away from the other person.
- Use clear, uncomplicated, deliberate movements and gestures.
- Pack your things calmly and deliberately when you exit. If you're a woman, turn and smile as you leave.

Technique 22. How to Handle Criticism in Business
- 'Put the Boot on His Foot' and ask the person what he would do if he was in your situation and someone criticized his company.

Technique 23. The Most Commanding Way to Answer the Telephone
- Make your name the last word the caller hears and use a Rising Terminal.

Technique 24. How to Give a Reprimand or Critique
- Use the 'Sandwich Technique'
- Criticize the act, not the person
- Ask for their help
- Admit that you once made a similar mistake and give the solution
- Make the criticism once, and do it in private
- End on a friendly note

Technique 25. How to Give a Persuasive Speech

- Ho-Hum – open with a dramatic, riveting or humorous story, or statement.
- Why bring that up? – tell your audience why you made the statement and why it's important to them.
- For example? – give three powerful points and three supporting points for each main point.
- So what? – motivate your audience to take the action you're suggesting.

Technique 26. How to Use a Visual Presentation

- Showing people things and getting them involved as you present ensures the maximum retention of what is said
- Use the *Power Lift* to raise their eyes so they can *see* and *hear* what you're presenting

Technique 27. How to Decide Where to Sit in an Interview

- Avoid the Competitive/Defensive sitting position.
- Jockey for the Co-operative or Corner Positions

Technique 28. Body Language – Ten Strategies that Give You the Winning Edge

- Keep your palms visible
- Keep your fingers together
- Keep your elbows out
- Keep your distance
- Mirror their body language
- Match their speech rate
- Uncross all arms
- Touch their elbow
- Repeat their name
- Avoid face touching

Conclusion

How to Train an Elephant

Have you ever noticed how circus elephants are tethered by a light chain that is attached to a steel spike driven into the ground?

A young elephant would have no difficulty pulling the spike out or breaking the chain, yet fully-grown elephants make no attempt to escape. Why is this so?

When they are young, baby elephants are shackled for hours every day by a strong chain around their leg to a large block of concrete by a strong chain around their leg.

No amount of pulling or tugging, squealing or trumpeting will set them free. As they grow older, they learn that no matter how hard they try, it's impossible to break away from the chains. Eventually, they stop trying.

They are now mentally conditioned to believe that when a chain is placed around their leg and tethered, it's impossible to escape, no matter how light the chain or how it's anchored. If a chain is attached, they're imprisoned.

From the day we are born, we are also conditioned by our trainers. Apart from our natural instincts, we arrive with zero knowledge and everything we do or think is a result of conditioning by 'trainers' – our parents, siblings, friends, teachers, advertisements and television. Most conditioning is subtle and repetitious and enters our subconscious to be stored for decision making at a later time in our lives. While some of this conditioning is designed to keep

us safe, much of it stunts our personal growth. We become tethered by mental and emotional chains. .

Our parents tell us *'Children are to be seen and not heard'*.
Our teachers tell us *'Only speak when you're spoken to'*.
Our friends tell us *'Never leave a secure job'*.
Society says, *'Pay off your mortgage and save for retirement'*.

The media tells us we're not good enough. To be happy, we must be slim, have perfect skin, hair and teeth – and smell sweet.

Their warnings are subtle and repetitious and become part of our belief system. As we grow through the steepest learning curve in our life, we are continually told what we *can't* do rather than what we *can* achieve.

Just as the elephant is conditioned to believe it can't escape, we can easily become 'can't do' people, restrained from success by repetitious negative conditioning.

The Displacement Approach

Imagine your current habits and attitudes about life are like water in a bucket. The bucket's contents have largely been filled by others – our parents, teachers, peers and the media.

Imagine now that each new skill and positive approach you've learned in this book is a pebble that you will drop into the bucket and that the water displaced represents current negative habits and attitudes. Eventually, the pebbles will displace most of the water and your bucket will be full of the positive skills, attitudes and habits that will serve you well throughout your life.

This book has given you the pebbles you'll need to relate with others on a high level, to become a more interesting, influential, magnetic person and to help people reach positive decisions. Take one skill each day and practice it until it becomes a part of who you are. It takes 30 days of repetition to form a new habit and make it permanent.

Start *now* to replace negative restraints with positive habits. How do you achieve this? The same way the elephant was trained; by repetitious learning, by continually practicing *positive* actions so that they become 'can do' habits.

References

Pease, A & B., *The Definitive Book of Body Language,* Pease International 2005,

Pease, A.V., *The Hot Button Selling System*, Pease Training, 1976

Pease, Allan & Garner, Alan, *Talk Language,* Pease International, 2004

Pease, Allan & Barbara, *Why Men Don't Listen & Women Can't Read Maps*, Pease International 2001

Pease, Allan & Barbara, *Why Men Don't Have a Clue & Women Need More Shoes*, Pease International, 2006

Pease, Allan & Barbara, *Why Men Can Only Do One Thing at a Time & Women Won't Stop Talking*, Pease International, 2003

Pease, Allan, *Questions are the Answers*, Pease International, 2003

Pease, Allan & Barbara, *How to Remember Names & Faces,* Pease International, 1996